REDISCOVERING FAMILY

Geoff Dench

HERA TRUST

First published in 2003
by the *Hera Trust*

18 Victoria Park Square
London
E2 9PF
UK

fax. 020 8981 6719

Copyright © Geoff Dench

The rights of the author
have been asserted in accordance with the
Copyright, Designs and Patent Act of 1988

All rights reserved

ISBN 0 9523529 3 1

Printed in UK by
Antony Rowe Ltd, Eastbourne

Cover design: Nick Green

[Cover portrait: Maria Paroissien
of Canrobert St, Bethnal Green]

Acknowledgement

The Hera Trust is grateful to the *Mutual Aid Centre* for its generous support of the Trust's publication programme.

Contents

Introduction:
A decade of rediscovery — 1

1 Reviewing sexual contracts — 7

2 Motherhood and the spirit of socialism — 27

3 Reversing the descent of man — 41

4 Full circle in the sexual revolution — 53

5 Men, families and careers — 71

6 Fathers, holy fathers and the spiritual dimension — 89

7 The importance of grandmothers — 97

8 Grandparents are back — 107

References — 141

Introduction
A DECADE OF REDISCOVERY

This volume brings together a number of short items that I have written concerning family and domestic relationships over the past few years, including some that are not currently in print. They span a decade during which I was gradually becoming drawn into this area of work. Looking at them now I am conscious that the earlier pieces, in particular, seem to have either a tentative or impulsive character, and certainly not authoritative, which presumably reflects the exploratory mood in which they were written.

The last ten years have witnessed a remarkable flowering of interest in the family. When I started writing the *Frog Prince* book (from which the first chapter here *Reviewing Sexual Contracts* was a left-over fragment) early in 1993, there was a good deal of debate taking place about sexual relations, patriarchy, New Man and that sort of thing. But hardly anyone referred to families. These were still seen by too many people in Britain as part of men's armoury of dirty tricks, contaminated in the sex war, to be a safe topic for public discussion or even academic analysis. Everything to do with them was fraught and bottled up. But it was not long after that, however, that family issues did start to break out, and soon surged into prominence again. It was as if, in my own perception at any rate, people had suddenly realised that the restraining hand of doctrinaire feminism was losing its grip, and could no longer persuade them that it knew what they felt better than they did themselves.

Around that time Lynne Segal wrote an article in the Guardian reassuring women that it was alright to enjoy sex, and to like men. A few years earlier this might have been greeted with a chorus of gosh, thanks Lynne. But in fact hardly anyone noticed. They had moved on from sex, and were talking about families. It had become possible again to think what you wanted, and to say what you actually thought.

Looking back, I am inclined to interpret this mass break-out as being linked to life-cycle developments, and the build up of related pressures. Part of this, obviously, is the motherhood thing. Early in the 1980s statist feminism had established a virtual monopoly in Britain of public declarations concerning what women wanted. As a result, increasing numbers of young women had been persuaded that work was far more important and rewarding than bringing up children, and that they should organise their lives around a career. By the mid-1990s this was routine; but it was already becoming harder to do. For one thing, biological clocks were ticking. The growing band of women prioritising careers had broadened into a column of lifestyle pioneers, pushing together deep into an uncharted future offering, for many, voluntary childlessness. But many were not light-hearted about this. Morale among the troops was shaky, and deserters were criticised heavily, indicating that it would not take much to prompt a stampede into eleventh-hour maternity.

The difficulties of prolonged denial, and maintaining a conspiracy of silence, were I suspect compounded by a less-obviously biological factor which, unlike it, would have been creeping up unsuspected. It may though have been even more influential in reviving interest in family life and motherhood - which in the last few years of the century duly re-emerged as if from nowhere to be reclaimed by many women as the key to their lives. The factor in question was that growing female investment in work may have changed the nature of the work experience. Prioritising career may be fun for women when they are only a minority of the workforce, but become less so when there are more of them. I have not seen this discussed anywhere, but it seems to me eminently plausible that women, especially younger women, are for a variety of reasons going to make more dramatic inroads in their chosen career if there are not too many other women to compete with. As the proportion of female workers increases, the character of the work experience changes.

Even *more* to the point, perhaps, as career women win their way through in greater numbers to senior positions, younger women entering work find that they have women on top of them as well as men. Much of the songsheet advocating the need to breach male monopolies then loses its pertinence. Even the notion of 'the career' itself may lose its shine, as female authority may not be so easy to challenge as male. What is the point of choosing a lifestyle where you can avoid being under the thumb of a mother-in-law if you then find that you have a female boss who has a similar authority over you and doesn't even have to get to know you and be nice to you. Family life in such circumstances may well come to seem preferable, and to offer greater real autonomy.

This brings us naturally to another life-cycle development which has stimulated and bolstered the family revival. That is grandparenthood. One of the most important factors prompting rediscovery of family life, and which has heavily influenced the direction of my own work over the last few years, is the finding of a voice by grandparents. During the 1990s a large number of 'sixties' girls started becoming grandmothers. They included many who had participated during their own youth in rolling the feminist revolution along, against the resistance of their mothers and grandmothers. They had no reason to feel intimidated by the current generation of activitists, and so were accordingly among the first to break the suffocating conspiracy of silence about family life.

What they have said strongly underlines its continuing centrality. Grandmothers have pointed out that in all historical periods women have chosen to do things other than just look after children, and that grandmothers themselves have always been the major support here. They have also reminded women that at the end of the day, and whatever the public message for that day, families *are* important to women. Many grandmothers have always given up or reduced their commitments in public life, to help look after grandchildren: not usually because they have to but because they want to. The new grannies are no exception. Having occupied a wider range of public roles than previous generations of women, and enjoyed them, current young grannies do still find the role delightful. And it is perhaps their discovery or rediscovery of this which has had the most decisive influence in banishing the idea that families and child-rearing are thankless tasks devised by men to keep women in bondage and out of men's business.

This opening-up of ideas which grannies have helped to promote came about very rapidly once it started. Turning over the Motherhood and Parent pages of today's broadsheets it is hard to remember that things were ever otherwise. But this does not mean that there is no longer anything to discuss. On the contrary, now that we are free to do so, there is a lot that needs very careful and, at last, very calm deliberation. It is this which makes it worth bringing these pieces together.

All have been used before. Full details of publications are given in footnotes on the first page of each chapter: but for purposes of exposition the main information is also outlined here. We are grateful to publishers of original versions for their co-operation in this.

Taking the items in order of appearance in this volume, 'Reviewing Sexual Contracts' came out in 1994 as a working paper of the Centre for Community Studies at Middlesex University. Some slight reformatting has taken place, leaving it a little shorter; but most of it is identical. The chapter 'Motherhood and the spirit of Socialism' first appeared as 'Tracking the Demeter tie', in the festschrift to Michael Young, *Young at Eighty*, published in 1995. The title has been changed in order to give a better idea of what it is about. No other changes have been made.

'Reversing the descent of man', was first published as a chapter in Trefor Lloyd's collection *What next for men?* in 1996, 'Completing sexual revolution' started out as 'Nearing full circle in the sexual revolution', in the collection *Rewriting the Sexual Contract* first published in 1997, and 'Men, families and careers', appeared in Yochanan Altman's *Careers in the New Millennium*, in the same year. A small amount of editing and reformatting has taken place for each of these.

The chapter 'Fathers, holy fathers and the spiritual dimension' was written for inclusion in the conference report *Fathers in the New Millennium*, which was to have been published by the Family Policy Studies Centre in 2000. This has been delayed by re-organisation of the centre's work. 'The importance of grandmothers', is an edited version of 'Why grandmothers?', the introduction to *Grandmothers of the Revolution,* published by Hera in 2000 and then subsequently republished by Transaction in 2002. Finally, 'Grandparents are back' first appeared in 2001, as a working paper for the newly-launched Grandparents Plus.

Incidentally, it may be worth mentioning at this point that careful readers may notice that in two or three places (e.g. between chapters 3 and 5, and chapters 7 and 8) there are pages of text which closely resemble pages elsewhere. They should not worry. These are not misprints. It is simply that things written for different purposes around the same time sometimes share a few discussion points. This sort of thing happens!

Lastly there is the matter of the book cover. This is most definitely a self-indulgence on my part, though not without its relevance and some piquancy. The photograph is of my maternal grandmother, dressed up for a formal portrait around her 18th birthday in the late 1880s. Why this is relevant is because of the way in which this image of her impressed itself on me in 1997, just around the time when families were starting to re-assert themselves again in the national consciousness and, even more tellingly for me, just after Michael Young had persuaded me to agree to carry out a national grandparenting survey. It all came about, moreover, entirely independently of my will.

What had happened was that during 1997 some papers filtered through to me following the death a few years earlier of an uncle.

These included this photograph of my grandmother, and her birth certificate. I had never met her, as she died a few years after my mother was born. I vaguely recalled, though had often forgotten, that one of the grannies I did know as a child – a rather solemn Frenchwoman who had come to England too late to perfect her English – was a *step*-grandmother. But I knew little about the missing blood grandmother. So I was more than mildly interested to read on this birth certificate that she had been born a few minutes walk from the Institute of Community Studies in Bethnal Green where I was working, and that the photograph had been taken in a studio in the road that my window there looked onto across the green. As I remarked to a colleague, it is one thing for a sociologist to dig around for roots, and quite another to have the roots come up and grab you by the ankle.

This coincidence ensured my commitment to the grandparenting study; and indeed to the Institute. You don't argue with signs like that. I knew already that my *paternal* grandmother had certainly grown up nearby – down towards the Mile End Road. So it now turned out that both had been East Enders and also, like my *step*-grandmother too, were Huguenots. If she had lived long enough it is not inconceivable that she could have become one of the Bethnal Green matriarchs encountered by Michael and Peter after the Second World War and immortalised in the *Family and Kinship* book. She missed that, and will have to be content with appearing on this book-cover instead, where she serves as a reminder that family is always there. We may forget family for a while. We may even deny it. But family does not forget us. It is liable at any time to pop up, when we are least expecting it, and when there are probably other things that we are trying to get on with, and insist that we rediscover it.

Ch.1
REVIEWING SEXUAL CONTRACTS[1]

Shaking the foundations

There has been a lively debate in recent years about the nature of relationships between men and women; and since the publication of Carole Pateman's influential commentary (1988) this has been seen by many as the most basic of 'social contracts'. I do not think this is the case. Those ties and reciprocal exchanges that take place between women - mainly as sisters, and as mothers and daughters - which help and constrain each of them to look after their offspring are logically and perhaps also historically prior to the social involvement of adult men. However, the regulation of relationships between men and women, specifying what they can legitimately expect from each other, are nevertheless pretty fundamental. They may be the key to successful building of all social structures beyond the most rudimentary levels. Certainly they mark a very significant stage in the development of social technology, and inform the concordat between private and public realms – the 'church' and 'state' as I suggest elsewhere[2] - whereby female-based moral communities license and recognise male-centred public domains.

These oppositions and resulting accommodations between realms are under attack at the moment - although the situation is confused as different people appear to take exception to

---

[1] This is an edited and slightly shortened version of a working-paper published in 1994 under the same title by the *Centre for Community Studies* at Middlesex University.
[2] Originally in Dench 1994. Edition now in print is Dench 1996a.

different aspects of them. Some women are hostile to the family and marriage on principle, as a restraint on their personal freedom. What others seem to object to though is the asymmetrical character of the gender relations which they see as flowing from its prevailing forms. If the elements of inequality could be removed or even toned down, so that men appeared more equally involved in and constrained by family obligations, then they could accept it all more readily for themselves. This is what many women now seem to anticipate when they refer to the need to renegotiate the sexual division of labour.

However, to phrase the issues this way around is I believe to raise false hopes in a most unfortunate and counterproductive manner. It is not a good starting point for a peace conference. Asymmetry in gender relations is not, I believe, the result of particular institutions. It is inherent in *any* partnership between men and women. Their basic interests and links with the community are so different that there can never be direct and simple exchanges between them. Patriarchy is not the enemy. It may even represent the main means of mitigating this original asymmetry – and arguably be the best mechanism yet devised for this purpose. Abandoning it probably makes it even harder for women to enjoy equal life chances with men. The asymmetry in cross-gender relations does mean that they are fraught with inter-personal difficulties. Nevertheless such relations do bring rewards to the communities which manage to promote them, both in general and to particular members. They elicit useful inputs from men to group life and also, perhaps even more crucially, reduce the problems liable to be caused by under-socialised males who are not properly incorporated into social life.

At a group level, then, sexual contracts produce obvious and reliable benefits in the effective management and control of men. For women as individuals, who are the points of contact with the community for the men in question, the balance-sheet may however be much more mixed. So there is a potential strain here between the interests of women as individual sexual partners, and as members of the wider receiving community. This strain is minimised where cultures explicitly emphasise difference and interdependence between men and women, and perhaps especially where women are excluded by social conventions from certain productive occupations. Such pluralism artificially boosts the utility of men as providers, and thereby women's individual incentives to sustain their ties with them.

Traditional sexual contracts can be seen as building on and extending the original social contract between women. In effect they require that in order to qualify for help from 'sisters' a woman does not merely need to take main responsibility for her own children, but should also accept a duty to the community to co-opt a man as her main provider. In this way her personal interests can come to coincide very closely with those of the community as a whole, of which she thereby becomes an active embodiment.

These traditional contracts appear to work well, and were adopted almost universally. This may be as they exploit men's and women's differences to make them dependent on each other - men on women for finding a place in society, and women on men for basic material supports - and play down direct competition between them. They recognise that men's and women's destinies, social positions, needs and possible fulfilment of social obligations have to be defined in different ways, and that no straight comparisons or common evaluation of them is possible. The resulting concordat accepts that there is men's work and women's. This intersects in the conjugal division of labour, between the outward-oriented breadwinner role and the inward-looking homemaker. But no common currency exists for transferring values from one domain to the other. It is possible to argue that this pluralism is itself unfair and restrictive and against natural justice. But so long as the dual system operates, partners cannot directly compare each others' performance. Each role is *sui generis*.

However, the balance of these structures is now under threat. Efforts made by contemporary feminists towards integrating realms of activity mean that criteria are being refined for directly assessing the relative contribution made by partners to their shared life. This deconstruction of separate realms, and replacement with unified sets of expectations, is I think a doomed exercise. For in the end the basic positions of men and women are, in fact, irreducibly and essentially so different. Much of the motivation to deny this seems purely ideological. It springs from a categorical refusal to accept that there are any 'givens' which communities cannot, or should not, move heaven and earth to ignore or redefine in a blind dash towards a universalistic vision of social justice. This is a seductive prospect, and the push to achieve it is causing tremendous mobilisation of energy and idealism. But I do not think that it is attainable. The foundations of social reciprocity are being shaken by determined efforts to draw up direct exchange rates, with strictly comparable obligations and performance indicators for both men and women. Sooner or later though something is bound to give.

Trading sex

To understand sexual contracts it is essential to remember that they occur between parties whose initial positions are poles apart, and who bring very different resources into the negotiation. Men enter such contracts as relatively free individuals, acknowledging few moral claims on themselves. They may be very marginal to the moral community, although quite possibly aware of its benefits and starting to become interested in moving into it. But the most compelling factor leading them into a relationship is not usually this. It is simply their desire for sex.

For women on the other hand, even in contemporary society, there is nothing at all simple about sex. It is potentially liable to result in the creation of new people for whom the woman, unlike her male sexual partner, would automatically acquire and feel a major responsibility. Because of this women have been infinitely less well placed to negotiate partnerships as autonomous individuals. They are far more concerned with the interests of existing or anticipated dependants, principally their children, and are also constrained by existing moral commitments to others in the community - their (female) partners in the original social contract whose support is or will be needed in helping to cope with motherhood.

All of this has to be taken into account when entering into a sexual relationship. A woman's own desire for sex herself may not come into it, though it has more play in post-pill society now that anxieties over pregnancy can be reduced. But sex is a consideration which she may well have to relegate to secondary importance. Much has been written over the last couple of decades about women 'faking' sex, a term which covers a range of behaviour. They all seem to revolve around the problem that a woman cannot afford to allow too much importance to her own inherent sexual desires, whatever these may be. To do so can reduce her ability to look after the interests of those in the moral community to whom she has obligations. As Mary Batten makes clear (1992) you cannot both prioritise sexual desire while at the same time bargaining with sex to maximise other possible benefits from a relationship.

Both men and women may be seeking sexual satisfaction for themselves and each other. But women will be much more aware from the outset of wanting more than just a simple exchange of pleasure from the relationship – and also be under greater community pressure to demand it. A straight trading of sexual servicing can rarely be enough for them. I imagine that this is why women have to play sex down. Modern discussion about faking refers mainly to pretending to enjoy it. But traditionally women had to pretend *not* to. So there is a tendency in all cultures towards treating sex as something which is much more important to men and which women will allow to them in rather particular circumstances - as a special and one-way gift requiring a whole galaxy of supplementary return gifts from men such as attentiveness to women's wider needs, plus provision of material supports, and general conformity with appropriate rules laid down by the community.

So the manoeuvring which takes place around sexual relations uses a woman's sexuality to pull men more fully into the moral community, on terms advantageous to it and, through this, to herself. Within this game the power of women is based on being *insiders* to the community controlling the terms by which men can enter to settle down and mature into responsible and rounded beings. It operates to focus community sanctions on the relation rather than in women as individual sexual partners. The power of men on the other hand does not depend on community support. It rests with their greater freedom as individuals. They are able in the last analysis to decide whether or not to accept admission to the community on the terms offered, and retain some residual capacity to pull out and disappear if they feel entrapped or if the arrangement ceases to provide enough inducements for them to stay.

Thus women collectively have the more powerful part in setting the rules for sexual relationships. But it is men who more often keep the interpersonal initiative and who will not bother to come in at all unless given adequate domestic privileges. So in many respects women cannot win. Sexual divisions of labour need to give privileges to men against their partners, in order to draw them in. For women it is therefore Hobson's choice. Either there are lazy or bossy men hanging around in the kitchen, posing problems for women individually. Or there are troublesome men roaming on the margins of society, creating difficulties for the community, and thus for women, as a whole. Nor, for all the centrality for men of biological drives, does sex need to take up much of their time. If access to women becomes hedged around too much by obligations, or guilt, then self-sufficiency is always at hand. Phillip Larkin's celebrated dictum in praise of onanism, to the effect that it saves both the expense of a night out and leaves one with more time for oneself, shows that what many men require does not call for a complex relationship, or indeed contract at all.

Even where men cannot handle this by themselves, it does not actually need a vast army of women to do it for them, if that is all that takes place between them. Prostitution is the bane of the moral economy. It undermines the bargaining power of women, by offering a quick and commitment-free alternative which corresponds rather too closely for comfort to a raw 'male' definition of what the exchange is really all about. Within many patriarchal societies a good deal of moral energy is spent in crusades against prostitution, ostensibly to save the women who are selling themselves. But the main point of it all may largely be to protect the long-term moral investments of respectable married women.

Marriage and the sex trade

It may not always be like this. The so-called matriarchal cultures - which many believe to have preceded patriarchy, and which have been identified through sexually-explicit 'goddess'-type cult artefacts - might well have involved more limited relationships between men and women that were closer to prostitution than marriage. Men who do not accept long-term commitments and responsibilities will nevertheless make some offerings in return for sex, on a piecemeal basis. This may be how it all began.

Even in fully-developed patriarchal society the pattern of material providing causes difficulty to some people in distinguishing between marriage and prostitution - especially perhaps to men who understand or care little about the moral economy. I was interested to notice, during a recent television documentary on the operation of the *Child Support Agency*, that some women are reluctant to ask for child maintenance payments from absent fathers of their children, because the men would regard such payments as entitling them to ask for sex with them. Thus the conjugal payment, seen by women as housekeeping money, and for bringing up the kids, may be regarded by many men primarily as a payment for sex. This is clearly why some married women feel themselves to be regarded by their husbands as not much more than prostitutes. In such an uncaring world it is obviously still important for many women not to enjoy sex, or to fake *not* enjoying it if necessary, in order to retain any bargaining position at all.

No doubt a socio-biologist like Helen Fisher (1993) would regard this type of relationship as quite acceptable to women, and as offering them the chance to increase their security by spreading their dependence over a number of male providers simultaneously. If some of them disappear, others will be left. This is perhaps why during periods of social upheaval, as during wars or great population dislocations, women may openly maintain a plurality of sexual partners in order to hedge their bets. But in less volatile situations where accidental deaths are quite rare the better strategy, and the one which pre-feminist cultures mainly seem to enjoin, is to seek security via long-term relationships which differ clearly from prostitution by virtue of duration and strength of commitment.

If a system based on piecemeal payments were the main or routine sexual relationship in a society, it probably would not elicit very reliable or substantial male social contributions - at most Rosalind Miles' 'jobbing extras' (1986). And also I suspect that it would generate more conflicts between women. So once patriarchy had been invented there would have been definite advantages to social groups in adopting it, and in replacing matriarchs in the Cynthia Payne mould with something more akin to Mary Whitehouse. As a stage in the emergence of society it is eminently believable. But at the same time I think that one of the main ongoing problems for societies *since* then has been how to avoid slipping back into it.

There are therefore a whole armoury of strategies and tactics for pulling men in and keeping up their interest in longer-term commitments, which involve fuller exchanges. The main devices, which are needed now more than ever, and which I will briefly explore below, revolve around pre-emptive reciprocation. These entail giving *first*, in the hope of prompting a return later and perhaps in the process stimulating new needs which will make men keener and more reliable trading partners. Secondly they involve presenting as gifts to men things which women *would do anyway* - again in the hope of making men feel obliged to reciprocate. Alternatively this can involve pretending that those things which men do give to women are not really gifts at all - either on the basis that they are not of very great value to women, or that *men* gain more themselves by 'giving' them than women do by receiving. There are hazards in all of these tactics, and prices to be paid. But we know that they do work, and it follows that women should not abandon them too recklessly.

Pre-emptive reciprocation

There is I believe a strong but currently under-acknowledged element of pre-emptive exchange inherent in the emphasis attached to fidelity and exclusivity in most 'patriarchal' sexual contracts. For this typically imposes greater initial self-denial on a woman. She will normally be contracting into a relationship at a time when her position in the sexual market is relatively much stronger than her partner's, and when she could most easily find another one. Reproduction and childcare exact more of a physical toll from a woman than a man, so that her period of greatest sexual attraction is usually concentrated into a shorter span. Withdrawal from this strong market position into an exclusive relationship is effectively a gift by a woman to a man of 'the best years of my life'. Though this may not be presented as such at the time, it can be referred to by her later, when her market value has declined, and then turned into a powerful moral lever to bolster her claims on her partner for continuing loyalty in return.

The practice and celebration of fidelity can be a very useful investment for women. But it is important to manage it in a way which steers between opposing hazards. On one hand it is important not to encourage the idea that women have themselves 'sacrificed pleasure', which would blow the concept of sex-as-a-gift-to-men right out of the water. On the other, care is needed to avoid challenging the convention that men are in control, which would alert them into scrutinising all of the exchange-values that they are operating with. So the 'best years' argument usually takes the form of arguing *not* that women would have welcomed sexual adventures for their own sake, so much as that they have foregone opportunities to find a more suitable sexual partner, which is often used to imply, in a nice moral twist, more faithful.

In this way the burden of responsibility is kept on men, and in particular on *male* possession and competition. It is men's 'domination' of women which is conventionally defined as the force underpinning the emphasis on exclusivity in marriage. In this way the community's need to secure and produce supports for women by tying men down is neatly turned back onto men themselves, some of whom may actually then develop appropriately possessive feelings to correspond with public cultural definitions.

There is perhaps one sense in which men are visibly more jealous or possessive than women - though it is not what is usually meant by this, and is really more a case of male marginality lending itself to representation as power. That is, insofar as men tend to be less deeply committed to any one sexual partner they may be less willing to put up with disloyal behaviour, especially if they are being expected to submit to the same general rules themselves. Paradoxically they are able to demand more loyalty than women, *not* because they want it that much more, or even as much, but because they are in a better position to ask for it - precisely because their commitment to the relationship is *less*.

There is no contradiction between this and saying that where they are free to do so men would, and on the whole do, accept more readily than women a sexual regime which does not prioritise exclusivity. The greater promiscuity of gay men than women, in corners of the sexual market where community regulations have much less influence than individual predilections, surely confirms the nature of this difference.

The double standard

The conventional idea of male power and possessiveness is however very effective in putting as much responsibility for sexual regulation as possible onto men, who are usually suckers for any flattering ideas that they are in control. Even if men are tripped into knocking in a few own goals here, though, this is I think an even greater potential hazard for women. Strategies for steering men towards feeling obligated into sexual fidelity can end up effectively licensing the moral dualism under which men may, in practice, be allowed greater freedom than women.

For if sex is generally held to be a far more powerful imperative for men than women then it is clearly much more difficult to prevent men from falling from grace sometimes: if their impulses are so insistent, their occasional lapses are morally less significant. For women, if sex really is no big deal for them, then there cannot be that much excuse for their infidelities. So where these do occur they will be indicative of much more serious disloyalty than in the case of men. Insofar as they may be chief agents in establishing rules of fidelity to promote their own security, and in presenting these to men as tribute to male dominance and rights, women may therefore end up trapping themselves into sexual passivity. This may well be part of the price they have to pay collectively in order to exercise moral control within the community.

Giving too much

> She was the sort of woman who lived for other people. You could generally tell them by their hunted look. (C. S. Lewis)

This price is perhaps part of a more general problem for women in that a strategy of pre-emption always involves some risk of giving much more than is returned to them - even at the discounted rate allowed to men. There is here a gulf to be crossed between men and women, a serious culture gap, which is the source of much mutual suspicion and incomprehension. This can be dealt with relatively easily in a pre-feminist context, where the sexes are *seen* to be different. But as this cultural consensus is abandoned, failures of communication are multiplying and augmenting.

The nature of this gulf is as follows. As full and willing participants in the moral economy, women generally have a strong feeling that gifts have to be repaid. They tend to use them to build up their moral stock in the community. When men fail to respond to things which women do for them, such as directing sensitive and caring attention to their needs and interests, providing them with domestic comforts and services and so on, women may be inclined to think that it must be because the men are expecting or requiring even *more*. So women may continue to give, even though any reciprocations they do get are late, grudging, and pathetically small. The effect of such derisory repayments, if continued over time, is to reduce drastically the self-esteem of the women doing all the giving. They come to feel that their value must be infinitely less than that of the 'dominant' beings to whom they are paying such inflated tribute.

In reality their partners may see it very differently, and have done so from the outset. For as relative outsiders to the moral economy, and fearful of it, men are not well schooled in the arts of giving and receiving. Their instincts will often advise them simply to give and receive as little as possible, in order to limit what may be expected of them in return. When in doubt, say 'no'. I think this is a contributory reason why men are essentially unresponsive. Up to a point silence may be, as women obviously suspect, a strategy of playing cool in order to raise exchange rates further and get even better deals. This is consistent with the fundamental card held by men in the relationship game, of greater indifference and needing to be tempted more before making a deal. But this can only be a small part of it. This card would have no power unless it was based on a real disposition of men to avoid engagement and minimise commitment. Male unresponsiveness to women's initiatives is not primarily a bid to elicit more, or to assert power. It is essentially just an attempt to give less. Just as women offer much, in order to ask for worthwhile returns, so men ask for little, in order to keep a lid on their future moral obligations.

This situation is alright for women if they *see* it just as that, and so themselves offer less. A balance can be achieved. But if they interpret men's behaviour as though they were female too, and react to male indifference by giving even more of themselves, the relationship is bound to deteriorate. A man confronted by a woman who smothers him with attention will either just soak it up, and tell himself that she must be getting pleasure out of it (otherwise why is she doing it?) so that he is in reality giving to her just by letting her do things for him. Or he will feel obliged and irritated at the same time, enfolded and entrapped in debt, and may become terrified at the thought of what eventually may be expected from him in return. He may then consciously turn up his indifference further, in order to discourage her. This may then provoke additional bouts of prestation until her sense of personal worth eventually brings her to a halt or is itself destroyed by the escalation. In none of these scenarios is the man drawn gently and persuasively into the culture of reciprocity. Nor is a strong partnership created between mutually respecting equals.

Doing it 'for men'

A sexual division of labour *can* be a basis for making both men and women feel useful and needed. This is because it contains an overwhelming presumption of mutual interdependence, which is a powerful factor promoting long-term support and commitment in relationships. The Victorian mother who reared sons incapable of feeding or clothing themselves did not see herself, as later generations of women have retrospectively cast her, as a slave to the idea that women should service men. She was turning out men who were *dependent* on women. She was engaged in keeping up the value of women to men other than just as sex objects, and through this ultimately the power of the community over men.

The notions of interdependence and exchange which accompany this traditional division of labour are not symmetrical. They are however flexible enough to allow satisfying and meaningful motivations to most of the people involved in them. The private realm of domesticity and family life is conventionally seen in terms of housekeeping and reproduction performed by women for particular men, in response to male will and desire, and in return for material support. The public realm of state and market affairs on the other hand is regarded as operated by men in return – both on behalf of particular women and their families *and* the (female) community generally.

A reasonable balancing of reciprocal servicing can be achieved within this model. This may depend though on retaining the traditional conventions of putting greater emphasis on male volition and subjectivity than on female, certainly at the interpersonal level of analysis. Where men do take on the role of family provider then this is seen as a matter of their personal choice in that they can avoid it, and could perhaps serve the community more directly, if they want to. A woman on the other hand is regarded as having a much smaller area of personal choice. By accepting a husband (or, more to the point, being 'given in marriage') she becomes obliged to do things as he decides and decrees, and much of her subsequent life is formally definable as doing things for him. Both of these ways of looking at the relationship can I believe greatly increase men's feelings of responsibility, and obligation, which in turn make *them* more amenable to control by others.

It is true that if the formal patriarchal conventions are taken too seriously a lot of bad faith is generated. Men's will becomes grossly overestimated, and identified with things which would happen, and women might want to do, anyway. And this is not just an occasional matter of houses being kept spotlessly clean in the name of men who really could not care less (but are afraid of appearing disdainful if they say so). Much more fundamental and binding issues are involved. Most women, even during supposedly dark Victorian periods, and presumably even under the most relentless ayatollahs, if only one could penetrate the thick layers of defence and ideology, have their own strong purposes in life which they can help to pursue by deploying shibboleths about male rule and control.

Most women, for example, do actually want to have children. The idea that this is something done for men, a gift to a husband (and even parents) and that it is the man who must decide when a child should be conceived and so on, is a way of putting responsibility onto men and drawing them at the same time into the moral community. An image of women as passive vessels awaiting injections of male desire and control is a very effective mechanism for harnessing male universalist spirit and converting it into particular flesh. At the end of the day most women get the children they wanted, and most men are tamed and domesticated into thinking that they wanted it and willed it. The female purpose, George Gilder would say, has successfully channelled the male energy.

Much of this deception is conventional, in that many traditional women recognise that patriarchal models offer only a partial account of the relationship between men and women. Countless Mary Dalys see that the hype does not work its magic on all men; and also (as she herself seems *not* to) that its final movers may not be male themselves. Pre-feminist women had a range of alternative, sub-cultural understandings, which encompass awareness of female influence behind the patriarchal veil, and the dependence of some men on women (as in 'men are all big children really'). These compensate for the formal emphasis on male will, and sustain women's own self-esteem.

I suspect that it is the flexibility given by these non-patriarchal ideas - which have been found among women in most surviving societies, and which feminism itself often builds on - which in the end square the circles of mutual interdependence and cancels out ostensible asymmetries. The idea of male subjectivity and 'doing it for men' is asserted at a public level. This is what steers men into serious acceptance of obligations. But then less formal and more realistic notions of male weakness or gullibility are available to protect women against the damage to their self-respect which can be caused by operating for long periods in patriarchal mode.

It is this balance which, paradoxically, is now threatened by feminist withdrawal of legitimacy from the male 'main provider' role, and the transfer of a residual provider role to men collectively via the patriarchal welfare state. For once women stop servicing men as individuals they lose touch with the concrete relationships through which they can see that real men don't actually fit the conventional stereotype at all well. Men themselves become deprived of their own sense of being needed, and learn that they don't need women either. Modern independent women soon create independent men. Equilibrial patterns of sexual reciprocation, and with them the chains of interpersonal interdependency and effective means of female control over men, dissolve into faint historical memories.

Giving and taking

Sexual contracts written around a division of labour bind men and women together. In the past they drew attention to mutual dependence, provided alternative and complementary accounts of who was giving and taking what, and avoided delicate questions about exchange rates by putting emphasis on equity rather than strict equality. But feminists have been trying to replace these with an entirely new formulation, the new man equation, which rejects the whole basis of conjugal reciprocity as previously understood. Several major consequences flow from this attempt to replace traditional conjugal exchanges.

The fundamental change offered by feminists lies in declaring that it should be a thoroughly symmetrical exchange, and that it is no longer legitimate for men to trade off the 'working for family' idea in the public realm against personal services in the private. Some parity is now required in each. The immediate effect of this change is to remove 'providing' from the account altogether, or possibly even to redesignate it as a debit rather than a credit. That is, a man who sees himself simply as a main provider is not regarded as giving anything to his partner. On the contrary, he is 'taking' the status and opportunity for self-fulfilment available in the public sphere, and hogging it for himself. If he wants to 'give' in this currency, he must be willing also to share his breadwinning role with his partner.

It follows from this that in order to get into overall credit men have to take on a good share of domestic activities, otherwise all of the giving will be seen as done by their female partners. This is why so many sociological studies of domestic activity in the last fifteen to twenty years have concentrated almost exclusively on the issues of who does which chore. These are the only things which count any more. Researchers are suitably brisk with respondents who show any sympathy with outmoded sexual divisions.

I think that it is becoming increasingly urgent to launch a new wave of research in this area to explore not simply who does what in the home, which we now know a lot about, but also which partner people think should do what, and why, and above all what they see as the *implications* of this. It would surely discover that fewer women than supposed have much confidence in the new man formula, either as something that is possible or even necessarily as equitable.

By concentrating on domestic labour, and equating equity with equality, it is very easy to score points and show that marriage is unfair to women. But many women, I believe, do remain committed to the institution because they feel that as a long-term arrangement it does suit their purposes, both as mothers and as citizens. As mothers they welcome a male companion and helper through most of their lives, and are prepared to do most of the domestic work - and pay the fidelity price - in return for this. As members of the community they recognise that men need to be domesticated in this way, and that women who take on a share of this work consolidate their own moral position in the community as a result. Contemporary studies of give and take in marriage ride blindly over most of these larger questions, in their drive towards a New Jerusalem of strict gender equality.

There are some tentative signs that the views of ordinary women are being heeded more now than a few years ago. Members of the Labour Party's *Commission on Social Justice*, on their journeys around Britain, have been discovering from many women that the problem with men these days is not just that they don't want to give very much, which always was the case. What is new is that now they don't seem to want much done for themselves either. Male indifference is at last being noticed. The domineering husband is gradually being replaced in popular demonology by the feckless but sexually independent drone. Earlier feminist canards about male control, and how to get a better deal by turning him into a sharing new man, are starting to come home to roost.

This has taken a long time to begin, and the women who have been paying the price in the meantime are not the ardent feminists in teaching and social services, who have had a good time on the whole. The ones who have lost out are those who have wanted to believe in marriage, but who have found that feminised state policies, geared to combating male oppression and to promoting female independence, have opened wide the doors to male irresponsibility. This has always been the main enemy of female security. During the last generation however it has effectively enjoyed the endorsement of the most vocal and influential sectors of female opinion, and has become common throughout British society.

That is the danger. Recently there are signs that this has started to shift again. Women's views seem to be becoming more mixed. There is greater willingness evident to consider non-statist propositions. A genuine and realistic debate with men, to renegotiate and update the sexual division of labour, may be at last becoming a serious possibility. So over the next few years it will be interesting to see whether the market is more open and responsive than, of late, it has seemed.

Ch.2
MOTHERHOOD AND THE SPIRIT OF SOCIALISM[1]

The main consideration prompting Michael Young's decisive step in the early fifties, away from the world of party politics into that of independent social research and commentary, was his concern that the essential roots of social life were being overlooked by policy-makers. Too fascinated by the marvels of economic growth and technological innovation, they were carelessly undermining the very communities which state machines derived their ultimate legitimacy by serving. What I want to suggest briefly here is that an important aspect of this concern was awareness that what was being neglected was the feminine aspect of society and the private realm informed by it.

Michael has attempted to conceptualise this through the idea of the Demeter tie, a special bond between mothers and daughters; but that concept has yet to make its full mark. This is something which the Labour Party in particular has continued to ignore, and it still has much to learn from his understandings if it is to cope successfully with the massive social transformations taking place in the last part of this century.

Michael's early writings on social policy show that he regarded a key function of the welfare state as compensating for the inadequacies and unreliability of men as family breadwinners, by providing direct benefits to mothers and their families. He was at one with earlier social reformers like Seebohm Rowntree in seeing the selfish behaviour of husbands as the cause of a great deal of

---

[1] This appeared originally in 1995 as 'Tracking the Demeter Tie', in *Young at Eighty,* edited by Dench, Flower & Gavron, and published in Manchester by Carcanet.

hidden poverty, and was influenced by the wartime studies of Charles Madge (who later played a valuable role in helping set up the Institute of Community Studies), indicating that a woman's personal dependence on her husband rendered her 'the lowest paid, most exploited worker in the country, given a mere subsistence wage, with no limit on hours worked'. (Madge, 1943: p.53.)

Michael believed that the welfare state could best liberate women from this, while supporting them in their domestic labour, by extending to them full citizenship rights in their own right. So he was an ardent supporter of Eleanor Rathbone in her campaign for family allowances payable to wives rather than husbands. On a number of occasions (e.g. 1952: p.313) he has quoted from her decisive contribution to the famous 1945 Commons second reading, to the effect that:

> If the money is given to the mother, and if they know that the law regards it as the child's property, or the mother's property to be spent for the child, that will help them to realise that the State recognizes the status of motherhood.

In large part it was this vision of the welfare state as a vehicle for helping virtuous mothers to become less dependent on tyrannical and uncaring husbands which fed Michael's growing dissatisfaction with the Labour Party. The trade unionist element was reluctant to weaken the concept of individual male breadwinners, whose family obligations gave moral legitimacy to their own economic demands. And the doctrinaire radicals were so obsessed by the primacy of the public realm, and issues like nationalisation, that they had little time to think about families and interpersonal relationships.

The resulting narrow pre-occupation with economic issues, which arguably produced the soil for second-wave feminism to develop in Britain, offered little scope for Michael's more pluralist and traditional world view - in which the link between public and private spheres mirrored and wrote large those between men and women, with women located at the communal hearth, nurturing children and cultivating civilised values, while men ranged around outside as their material supporters and agents.

Michael noted appreciatively at the end of the first Labour administration that the welfare state, through family allowances, school meals, milk and food supplements and the NHS had done much to cushion women against male derelictions of obligation, and to redistribute resources discreetly from men to women. 'In general it is as though the taxes on tobacco and drink had been paid into a family income equalisation pool, from which had been drawn the benefits provided by the State.' (1952: p. 319) But he was feeling that much remained to be done, and in his penultimate policy discussion paper as an employee of the Party he made a final plea for more to be done for mothers.

> It is a remarkable fact that it was not until the election of a Labour Government in 1945 that anything effective was done to ease the strain of modern living on the ordinary, workaday family ... (This precedent) we should prepare to follow when next a Government is elected responsive to the needs of the people, responsive, above all, to the needs of the mothers in whose arms the future rests. [Adding with resignation] I herewith pass the baby to the National Executive Committee. (1951: p.1)

Motherhood and community

So Michael's escape from the prison of Left thought and his journey with Peter Willmott into the East End - a region long toured by reformers and social enquirers eager to witness at first hand the effects of male moral weakness - has to be seen I think as already mapped out by an interest in the value of women's labour. But the exuberant social reporting which then followed in *Family and Kinship in East London* suggests that even Michael was taken back by just how central women proved to be. For it was Mum who emerged as the undisputed heroine of that study. Motherhood was revealed not just as child-rearing - much as that undoubtedly was - but also as the linchpin of community itself.

Childrearing is such a relentless burden that women could not manage without mutual support and reciprocity, and the interpersonal exchanges and obligations which they arranged between themselves were the principle content of extended family networks, general neighbourliness, and an open school for learning key moral values upholding mutual aid and interdependence. The central co-operative relationship in this structure was that between mother and daughter, which combined a long-term and morally inescapable mutual indebtedness with a convenient asymmetry and compatibility of age, experience and availability. As Michael and Peter put it:

> And so it goes on - the daughter's labours are in a hundred little ways shared with the older woman whose days of child-bearing (but not of child-rearing) are over. When the time comes for the mother to need assistance, the daughter reciprocates, as reported elsewhere, by returning the care which she has herself received. (1957: p.39).

It was through helping her daughters in this way that an older woman found herself becoming a pillar of the community, whether she wanted it or not, and a matriarch around whom the lives of younger generations revolved, and through whom people traced key relationships and placed themselves in the local community. It was Mum who slipped a fiver to the housing agent to secure a new tenancy, and whose home was the centre of the extended family, where her daughters gathered. She not only held the family together, but presided over the moral economy regulating ties with other families. There was no need to put her on a pedestal as the role she played put her there already. 'Since her status as 'Mum' is so high, it is derogatory to call her by any other name.' (ibid: p.33)

Just as community proved to be largely a matter of extended families, these themselves turned out to be almost wholly a matter of grannies. It is perhaps surprising that this analysis did not culminate in a double equation to the effect that $C = EF =$ Mum. Instead, and perhaps to avoid grappling directly with the paradox of why we should choose a term like fraternity to describe virtues which are characteristically taught and exemplified by women, the concept of (discreetly gendered) neighbourliness was invoked, with the formula, expressed most cogently in *The Symmetrical Family*, (1973: p. 287) that 'neighbourly socialism is the mother of political socialism'.

That it was mainly Michael who saw civic virtue as being grounded in the private realm, among women, and community as shared motherhood, is I believe confirmed by the gender dimension present in the *Rise of the Meritocracy* story, which he was writing at the same time. *Meritocracy* is notable for its ambivalence and irony: and this is why it has been read in different ways. But there is little ambiguity in its celebration of female values and activities. Thus within the clearly mixed attitudes towards family displayed in the story, it is not hard to discern that it is the male aspects of family, linked with inheritance, property and public position, which are portrayed as having anti-social implications, while the female side of nurturance and mutual support is affirmed as truly moral and socially integrative. The narrative itself can be read as a morality tale in which women are obliged to intervene in order to save the men who are supposed to be running the show from the consequences of the mistakes they are making. It suggests that women, as the guardians of the values on which social order and the legitimacy of the public domain ultimately depend, can withdraw men's licence when they lose their way.

For the emergence and rise of this meritocracy takes place as the men in charge of the state, perhaps a little like the leaders in

Attlee's postwar administration, forget the varied nature of social ends or purposes and get carried away by the pursuit of specific means - in this case super-efficiency of human resource development. The open and heartlessly universalistic competitiveness of this male system then leads towards instability and social division, as ever fewer people feel they have a stake in the system. Its days are numbered after women, beginning with those shaggy young girls from Newnham and Somerville, withdraw their support for the regime.

These female leaders of revolution have sometimes been identified as harbingers of second-wave feminism. But I think that claim is invalid. The politically effective women are clearly defined in terms wholly at variance with modern feminism, which mobilises around equal participation in the public realm, and in fact they have much in common with those women vilified by Faludi (1992) as collaborators with a (supposedly male) backlash. It is not that they are opposing the system because they are excluded from it. They defy it because they believe in community and its sacrificial heart, motherhood.

> The determination of so many of the present leaders of the movement to do all their own household work is unusual and in some ways welcome since it means the married ones have little time left over for political organisation.

> Through the women's circles, the activists have been able to assert their influence and show their menfolk, who perhaps show too little humility about the wonders with which they have furnished our estate, that they are a force to be reckoned with. In so doing they are making a protest against the standards, those of achievement, by which men assess each other. (1958: p.173)

The guiding spirit of the Populists is unveiled here as Nemesis, the ancient goddess of righteous wrath.

Demeter found, and lost again

Michael's sensitivity, in the face of conventional models, to what actually goes on in society was I think a major factor behind the massive popular success of *Family and Kinship*, and possibly to some extent of *Meritocracy* too. Most people experience intimations of matriarchy at frequent intervals: but as these are not endorsed by official culture they learn to ignore them or interpret them in other ways. *Family and Kinship* held up a mirror to everyday life which ordinary people recognised instantly and which encouraged them to realise that they did after all understand how the world worked. Bethnal Green served not just as a metaphor for unrepresented common man, but also for unreconstructed common sense: for a moment sociology and folk culture sang in harmony. The appeal of the book was very similar to that of modern soap operas now which, with the exception perhaps of Brookside, circumvent current orthodoxy by pretending that their portrayals of female centrality are merely fiction.

Not everyone approved of it of course. For most people it breathed fresh air into corners where stuffy dogmas had lingered too long. To an anthropology student like myself, reading *Family and Kinship* a couple of years after its publication, it came as a revelation that sociology did not have to be arid or divorced from real life. I then enthusiastically spent a good deal of my final year working with Michael to establish a student Sociology Society in Cambridge to spread the word, and soon changed disciplines myself. But for radical women setting out on the long march towards strict equality, family and motherhood were not fit objects of admiration, and many said so. Michael had been warned. While *Family and Kinship* was being written he had addressed the Town Planning Institute on the importance of protecting extended families, and in the ensuing discussion the redoubtable Ruth Glass had pointed out sternly that if relatives were the most important source of support at childbirth this should be seen as indicating a failure on the part of the social services to help families in coping with their everyday lives.

> [Moreover, she] did not think that one could regard the extended family as a substitute for a widening of the horizon of social responsibility ... Of course, we were all capable of sharing the joys and pains of members of our own family. But in the long run it was our ability to identify ourselves with the fate of adults and children further and even far away - for instance, with the experience of a few Japanese fishermen - which would count. It was the growing sense of interdependence with ever widening groups, indeed with humanity as a whole, which signified social progress. (1954: p.141)

This tone was echoed many times during the sixties, especially in the universities, by feminists (still almost entirely women) who thought that motherhood was just work like any other, and were convinced that the welfare state represented the long-awaited wand for banishing distinctions between public and private spheres. They resented what they felt to be a romanticisation by Michael and Peter of social arrangements which trapped women in domesticity. Quotations from old ladies affirming that 'With a daughter you've always got someone to ask' (1960: p.72) were instantly translated by them into 'As a daughter you can never say no', confirming that women lived in bondage.

What was perhaps even harder to swallow, I suspect, was that both *Family and Kinship* and *Family and Class in a London Suburb* (1960) revealed men as bit-parters and minor characters, hardly figuring in the central action. So these studies hindered the construction of a theory of imperious patriarchy in which men could be portrayed as the arch enemy: and this made it harder to mobilise female solidarity.

During the sixties Michael explored the idea of the mother-daughter relationship as a universal and fundamental element in social relations. He started referring to it as the Demeter tie, counterposing it against the Oedipal tie which the Left were fond of dwelling on as evidence of the primordial nature of patriarchy. But he had little response, and in his next (and final) book with Peter on family and gender, the *Symmetrical Family* (1973), gave in I think to critiques and pressures by choosing to explain the tie less in general terms of elementary interpersonal reciprocity, generated spontaneously within the private realm, and more in terms of particular changes forced onto family life by developments in the world of economics and politics: the 'four stages' theory. It was surely no accident that this doctored model appeared a couple of years after Jennifer Platt's *Social Research in Bethnal Green* (1971), which Michael and Peter reviewed, and which they acknowledged there as 'helping to clarify' their own emerging theory. Realism could not prevail against ideology in the longer run.

Michael withdrew from this arena as it became engulfed by sex war. In the conclusion to *Symmetrical Family*, which failed interestingly to repeat the popular impact of the earlier family studies, there are suggestions made that 'women liberationists' may soon provoke a reaction against themselves. Michael went on sniping gently for some years, complaining that Women's Liberationists were ignoring the problems of non-working women (1974), and warning that:

> Women out at work who do not have much time
> to spare for their mothers will, when they are old
> themselves, suffer likewise when their daughters
> follow their example.
> (1977: p.351).

But essentially he was shifting his major interest and activities to other areas, such as distance education in Africa, the co-operative movement, and the new Social Democratic Party.

So his analysis of the sexual constitution of society has been deferred. But I believe that it would almost certainly hinge on some fairly traditional separation of private and public domains, as spheres of principal engagement in society of women and men. That which he has written makes it clear that the private realm of interpersonal relations and exchanges revolves around child-bearing and rearing, where men cannot expect to play as full a part as women. The corollary of this would be that men are driven to make their main contributions and sacrifices in the public realm, as it is here that they are best able to repay their childhood debts to mothers and grandmothers, by labouring to exploit nature to social purposes, and through good works to ensure that moral values originating in the private realm are honoured and upheld in the public. Observation of Michael's behaviour certainly suggests that his idea of male destiny or calling focuses around the imagery of serving causes emanating from the community, especially women, though if possible without becoming too tied down in the process. The good knight, having fought a decisive battle and secured a position and resources for the infant cause and its committed carers, soon feels restless and finds himself pledging his last drop of blood to a new mission.

This pursuit of a good cause can be so enthralling for Michael that he becomes oblivious to the need for personal rewards of those serving alongside him. Not long ago I was sitting with him in a rush-hour traffic jam (why *won't* he travel by tube?) on the way to a meeting called to plot the creation of a new organisation. We were picking over some ideas to float, and I trotted out a number of suggestions that I had been peddling for several years. Michael turned towards me and said warmly, 'You know, some of your ideas seem to be catching on at last: a lot of people are starting to say the same sort of thing now.' I muttered something about how irritating it was that so few of them were giving me any credit for risking to say them before they became popular. 'Oh! come now,' he said reprovingly, without flickering, his eyes now locked firmly onto the tail of a stationary yellow Routemaster, 'that does not matter surely. What is important is that public opinion is moving in the right direction.'

Time for a new crusade

This also goes to show, I suppose, how Michael's receptivity to public mood informs his timing of action so effectively. When the current wave of feminism was at full flood he kept his head down and got on with other jobs. But since feminism has mellowed and become more divided on strategic issues and started to worry about possible unintended consequences of its own campaigns Michael has been feeling his way back towards his original causes.

Beginning with his ESRC lecture on the family (1990) and the work on after-school clubs (1992) which led to Education Extra, and then through the Family Covenant Association, designed to bolster parental responsibility, to his recent lobbying with Frank Field on family income and the related pamphlet with Chelly Halsey about Family Socialism, Michael has been plugging away again at his basic theme since leaving the Labour Party research department - that the central concern of social policy should lie in finding ways to support women and build families and communities around the essential work which women do, and of endorsing the Demeter tie at the heart of this.

Since Michael left its service, the Labour Party has travelled a long way down the very different road of dismantling sexual divisions of labour and complementarity of roles in favour of publicly regulated equal opportunities. It is perhaps difficult to envisage this Party now believing that there is anything to learn from Michael. But it is significant, I think, that just at the recent moment of triumph for Emily's List there should have been heard within the party the voice of a veteran campaigner for women's rights, Clare Short, warning young female careerists that it might be time to reconsider whether opening up the public realm too radically may not risk leaving men without a valued and distinctive role to fulfil.

Now that feminism has worked its way through the system and the fragility and artificiality of patriarchy is becoming evident, the hostile attitudes of the last two decades are dissolving. The idea of mothers as 'friends of the enemy' (Bunting, 1993) is giving way to rediscovery of the mother-daughter bond as a source of mutual support (Billington, 1994). So maybe enough women are now ready to embrace a Demeter concept, celebrating the collective strength of women and the moral centrality of the private realm, to allow serious renegotiation of roles with men at last.

It is not only the Left (virtually synonymous these days with statist feminism) which has much to learn still from Michael. I have written a good deal lately from a different perspective (most recently in *Transforming Men*) on the collapse in male motivation precipitated by de-gendering the public realm. And my main line has been to argue that men need to have some formalised priority in this domain in order to become responsible and productive members of society. But after considering Michael's latest ideas on family wages I can see that there are always several ways of approaching a problem, and that the direct line is not necessarily the best.

So, for example, instead of explicitly pushing the notion that men should normally expect to be main breadwinners in a household, why not just juggle with the welfare system to prioritise even further the rights and benefits of women, who perform most 'community' work, while stressing the citizenship obligations of men? In this way social attitudes will be encouraged to shift towards acknowledging both the value of caring activities to society generally, and also the need to provide paid work in order to elicit and organise a full contribution from men. This may be a better way to re-balance the spheres.

It is also more or less what Michael has always stood for. He has never proposed obstacles to women having paid jobs, and has himself employed disproportionate numbers of them to staff his empire. But he has not encouraged this at the expense of family work, and his advocacy of the welfare state in the forties was premised on an assumption of the primacy of caring work.

> Whatever the motives of the mothers, it is clear that the temptation (sic) for women to work outside the home will be stronger where their allowances are small. (1952: p.318).

These are ideas which have not been heard for years, and which some people thought not to do so again. But they will be aired increasingly, I believe, in the concluding turmoil of this millennium, as we grope our way towards a new sexual contract. Michael will be there in the thick of it all: he may at last find the opportunity in this to round out the Demeter concept. Even if he does not, his vision lights the way for others, and the reaction which it has provoked helps us to see more clearly the nature of the issues and forces that are involved.

Ch.3
REVERSING THE DESCENT OF MAN[1]

On virtually every indicator that anyone might want to consider, men in Britain and various other western states seem to be performing very badly at the moment, both for themselves and for the communities in which they live. And all the signs are that the situation stands to get much worse. What I want to argue here, however, is that this is to some extent not an unusual situation. Men everywhere are inclined towards being social outsiders. Their usefulness to communities varies much more than women's, and depends greatly on the way in which social institutions define and reward their roles. Whereas most cultures seem to recognise this, in the West we have increasingly pretended that it is not the case. And we are now paying for our mistake.

It is not too late to face up to the problem. But we have such an accumulation of policy errors to deal with that we require a thorough re-orientation of public discourse before we can expect any specific measures to have much positive effect. The sort of shift that we need encompasses a moral reinstatement of at least some key elements of the sexual division of labour, probably grounded in stronger marriage institutions, and certainly linked with a conceptual unscrambling of the private realm of interpersonal relations revolving around families, and the public realm concerned with the impersonal organisation of collective life.

I will start by discussing this broad cultural transformation before

---

[1] First published in 1996 in Trefor Lloyd (ed) *What next for men?* London: Working With Men.

sketching out some policy directions which would become feasible under it. My general approach may seem wildly speculative to some people. But I do actually believe it to be consistent with the way that public opinion is currently moving. Many people are asking themselves whether some of the radical social experiments attempted in recent generations are viable in the long term, or should now be ditched. Our journey along the path I am signposting may already be underway.

Recognising sexual difference

The first step towards pulling men back from their plunge into unproductive and anti-social behaviour patterns lies in acknowledging that the social orientations of men and women can never be identical. Refusal to accept this, and pursuit of interchangeability and strict equality rather than seeking more appropriate goals of gender *equity*, are likely to increase not to reduce social differences between the sexes.

The key to this is that women in all societies are more responsive to each other's needs, and to the value of a social contract. In the last analysis, this is because they need society more. The long and arduous process of child-rearing makes women become interdependent and value co-operation with others in a way which does not so readily apply to men, who can more easily get along by themselves and thus avoid commitments to others. Society is at heart female, and is built around shared motherhood.

In all 'traditional' cultures there is a more or less explicit awareness of the centrality of motherhood, and of the need to create similarly distinctive roles for men in order to give them a comparable stake in society. We all need to feel needed by others, if we are to learn to be responsive to them. Unless adult men are given clear roles and duties their attachment to society is very tenuous.

The highlighting of male roles which results, and corresponds broadly to what we call patriarchy, has two main aspects. Firstly, men are made socially responsible for the support of particular women and children, usually but not necessarily their sexual partners and own offspring. This makes men more like women, by giving them specific people to care about in the way that mothers have to care for their children. Secondly, they are given formal rights and duties, usually linked to a 'head of family' status, in the structure of political and economic institutions which organise access to the means of support. This increases their motivation and opportunity to carry out their family obligations.

As David Gilmore's cross-cultural study of men shows (1990), in the small handful of cultures without patriarchy men live a narcissistic Peter Pan existence, putting very little into the community and leaving most labour to women. Such societies have not developed beyond a rudimentary level, and cannot compete with more highly organised and structured neighbours. This is why there are so few of them. They are not a suitable model for modern industrial nations to copy.

Re-jigging equal opportunities

Copying them is, however, effectively what we have been doing in recent decades as attacks have mounted on sexual divisions of labour. Since the Enlightenment the philosophical doctrines of individualism have come into repeated conflict with ideas about sexual differences. During this century, as the state has offered increasingly direct supports to women, libertarians, especially in Protestant countries, have portrayed male providing roles as a major source of evil.

Eleanor Rathbone, for example, persuaded parliament in 1945 to by-pass husbands and pay family allowances to mothers, after conducting a long campaign against what she dubbed the 'Turk complex'.

> It is easy to see what satisfaction the institution of the dependent family gives to all sorts and conditions of men - to the tyrannous man what

> opportunities of tyranny, to the selfish of self-indulgence, to the generous of preening himself in the sunshine of his own generosity, to the chivalrous of feeling himself the protector of the weak. ... Thus when a proposal *(for direct state support of women)* presents itself which is obnoxious to the hidden Turk in man, he stretches up his hand from his dwelling in the unconscious mind and the proposal disappears from the upper regions of consciousness. (1924: p. 270-1)

Rathbone herself was mainly concerned with improving the status of motherhood, by defining it as a public role deserving direct state support. But her breach of the divide between private and public realms, and dismissal of male family motivations (but not of female) as rooted in an 'instinct of domination', contributed to a de-legitimising of distinctive male roles. It was a factor in the emergence of a new statist political economy in which segregated roles are deemed harmful to society and where men who still aspire to them are regarded as morally deviant or pathetic throwbacks.

This process has become intensified since the sixties, when the emergence of the pill, allowing much more reliable planning of families, encouraged women to start claiming equal participation in the formerly male-oriented public realm. This development has I believe been the clinching factor which decisively weakened the framework of family responsibilities which previously underpinned men's motivation to take on socially useful labour. Some of this is revealed in Neil Lyndon's retrospective baring of soul:

> If we didn't have to have babies when we had regular sex, it followed that we didn't have to get married. And if we didn't have to support families, we didn't have to have jobs or careers: and if we didn't have to have careers, ... what

might we not do? Or be? A *tabula rasa* of adult masculinity had been presented to us, upon which we might (we supposed) make our marks as we pleased. (1992)

It is now time to discard this legacy. I argue elsewhere (1994) that it has it led to a collapse not only in male participation in public realm activities, but in family work in the private realm too. Far from leading to a more equitable sharing of roles, it has piled ever greater burdens on women.

Policies of strict gender equality are no longer what most women want - if indeed they ever did. Many women, especially older women with experience of managing families, see some emphasising of men's economic roles as an essential basis for turning them into caring and productive members of the community. There is popular support building up for a reformulation of equal opportunities policies to allow for differential involvement of men and women in family life.

This might best be done by attaching greater importance among *younger* people to women's employment rights - as they do not have so long to establish themselves in work before wanting to give much of their time to running a family - while reserving priority among people *aged thirty or over* to men - who are often slower getting started anyway, but whom most women would in fact prefer to occupy the main breadwinning role during the arduous years of childrearing.

A formal shift of emphasis like this would signal to men that there are socially valued roles waiting for them, and offer reassurance and meaning in life to the growing numbers of them who seem to doubt it.

Prioritising male work

Heavy rates of unemployment are widely seen as related to the collapse of male morale and motivation. But it is a mistake to regard joblessness in itself as the cause of men's problems. Male unemployment is no novelty, and reached high levels as recently as the thirties without weakening male resolve and family commitment or readiness to retrain for new types of work. Arguably it even sharpened these.

What is new is the loss of morale and sense of purpose among men, and this is a cultural rather than an economic change, arising out of the libertarian assault on sex roles. Men are bombarded with the message that modern women value the opportunity for self-realisation through work. So the chivalrous thing to do these days (as Eleanor Rathbone was warned but chose to ignore) is not strive too hard to achieve and hold down a job, but to stand aside and let women go for it themselves. This is the root of contemporary male economic and educational failure, and the reason why, although there are increasing numbers of unemployed men, the total number of *jobs* remains the same.

It is not possible to do much about this so long as the problem is seen simply in terms of the amount of work available. Boosting employment in the current climate is likely to benefit women much more than men, as they are the ones presently more highly motivated (by existing or anticipated family duties) to take it seriously. We need measures which endorse the greater relative importance of work to men as their distinctive contribution to society.

One step which could be taken quite early on in a process of reasserting the value of male work and which would help start to rescue the self-respect of unemployed men is to change the *nature* of supports offered to men when they are out of work. All of the main political parties are developing schemes for limiting benefits to the unemployed, and replacing them with training schemes and job-seekers allowances of various kinds. But these all still rely on the private sector actually to create new work, while through taxation reducing its capacity to generate such jobs.

It would be more constructive, and no longer likely to incur union wrath, to replace benefits for able-bodied work-seekers with wages for socially useful work. In some circumstances this might be 'family work' of bringing up children, as proposed last year by Michael Young and Chelly Halsey (1995). Nominally this could be open to men or women, but in practice few men are likely to choose it or qualify for it. More significantly, in terms of getting the nation working again, it could be low-paid (or part-time) work in state enterprises.

This would initiate a valuable shift in the structure of public spending. Part of Britain's economic malaise derives from trying to incorporate too many personal services and supports, previously (and often better) carried out in the private realm, into the welfare state. This has burdened the welfare system far beyond its original remit, and has competed with the budgets available for stimulating industrial investment and modernisation. Focussing public monies into public works schemes could get resources circulating in ways which revived men's interest in working and supporting families at the same time as assisting industrial renewal.

Creating real work

Such a public employment system will only result in a re-harnessing of male energies if it offers real and useful work, and is concentrated in areas which do not require massive and sudden re-culturation of men. It must utilise currently wasted male labour, as well as helping to generate new jobs in the private sector - which in the last analysis is paying for it.

Many people will be shaking their heads at this point and chanting that 'traditional male work is in decline'. But this is not fundamentally true, and is a culturally-constrained perception, related to the attempt in the West to merge public and private domains, and to *pay* for caring work out of public funds. If we treat more personal services as private realm obligations (to be negotiated within families, or *paid for* by families) and then look for traditional 'work' there is plenty that still needs doing and could be paid for.

A new wave of public employment could be directed mainly towards renewal and maintenance of the infrastructure needed by a modern economy. For example, an efficient public transport and communications system, where public investment has been starved in recent decades, is a heavy consumer of traditional labour. Also the conversion of industry and agriculture to ecologically-sound techniques and practices, along with measures to clean up the existing environment, are essential to the long-term economic health and growth of the nation, and something which a progressive government should undertake. Such a programme would use massive amounts of labour, some of it perhaps organised into mobile task forces, and mainly of the sort towards which today's men are already oriented.

Public expenditure entailed would finance itself partly by the major reduction in direct payments of benefits to men; but there would also be direct and indirect gains from the associated slimming-down of welfare bureaucracies. People fit to work but unwilling to participate in public work schemes could be given the last-ditch defence of accommodation in hostels where most of the labour was provided by the residents themselves. In this situation people's family networks would soon re-emerge as valuable and valued sources of (reciprocal) supports, and this itself would help to further boost the importance of male 'providing' and thereby the private realm incentives available to men.

Reviving family networks

A general rebuilding of conventional families would produce, as Patricia Morgan's recent work shows (1995), a number of powerful reinforcements for men's morale. Restoration of tax incentives for marriage would reduce the perverse incentives to family breakdown and male abdication which are created by the present benefits structure, and steer caring work back into the private realm where it helps to stimulate reasons for men to work.

Single people, in particular single childless men, should be taxed at a much higher rate because they are less likely to be engaged in the reciprocal support activities of the moral economy which limit the collective liabilities of the welfare state.

The proposals outlined here may be dismissed out of hand by some people on the grounds that they would push women back into domestic labour. But I would argue strongly that they need not have this effect, and do in fact represent an updating of patriarchy with which most women would already at some level agree. It is in any case absurd to talk of pushing women back into kitchens, because the vast majority have never left, and still do by far the larger share of domestic work even where they do have partners. Domestic liberation of women is due more to technology than to help from men, which is largely mythical, and insofar as it does exist is positively, rather than inversely, related to a man's breadwinning status. Men reasonably successful at work and able to contribute to families through this are also *more* involved than others in domestic chores (Dench, 1996b).

Male breadwinning is turning out not to be the enemy of modern women. Once they have children, most women would actually prefer a male partner to carry the main economic burden, while themselves performing the main family management and caring role. That this is not more widely understood is largely due to the personal inclinations of most social researchers and commentators, who are at variance with the bulk of the population. Recent research that I have participated in myself suggests very strongly that not only are most women in favour of an up-dated sexual division of labour but that support for it is growing steadily at the moment, especially among mothers.

Women, who when younger may feel that equal participation in the public realm is essential to their self-respect, change their minds as their own children grow up and they find themselves becoming the linchpin in a wider family system. They are concerned at their sons' lack of motivation, at the shortage of suitable partners for their daughters, at the polarisation among younger people (between civilised women and increasingly uncivilised men, who find it hard to live together and even harder to stay together) and at the distress caused to children and older people too by the general weakening of family networks.

Redistributing employment

There is a strong class dimension to the problem of modern men, as the de-motivating effect of equal opportunities rhetoric does not affect all men equally. It is regressive in class terms. As the male provider role fades as a source of respect in wider society, men who can only realistically hope for low status work are the ones most likely to lose the will to seek jobs or retrain as old industries decline. Middle class men with more chance of interesting and prestigious jobs have incentives to succeed which need less boosting by family obligations. So they are not held back in the same way.

I believe this is a powerful factor sharpening the polarisation of our society into rich and poor sectors. The division is increasingly between an elite of 'two-career' families who live in affluence, and an underclass of 'no-work' families - or rather non-families, as it is mostly within this section of the population that households are breaking up, with men increasingly unemployed, living alone, dying of self-neglect and losing faith that there is a useful place for them. Women in this underclass suffer great stress and poverty too, but they keep going because they know that they have valuable roles as mothers.

Taxation policy could play a significant role here in averting broader social conflict at the same time as re-motivating men. Dual-earner households enjoy a disproportionate share of jobs, incomes and also of valuable incentives. There is much in their lifestyle that is against the common good, as they have augmented everyone's cost of living by taking out double-salary mortgages which inflate the general level of house prices, and have helped to undermine family life by pressing for separate taxation of domestic partners. In spite of sometimes hiding behind leftish politics, they are the essence of two-nation Thatcherism. High combined taxation of working couples is needed to compensate for the social costs to the community generated by such households.

Redeeming the hidden Turk

Eleanor Rathbone was undoubtedly right in assuming that many men draw great strength and satisfaction from the idea that they are playing an important role in supporting families. What makes her position and the dismantling of sexual divisions of labour which draws on ideas like it so wrong-headed, even prissy, is the idealistic judgement that this renders men unacceptable. In the last analysis any society depends on this type of reward structure and motive.

Throughout history communities have found that the most effective way to lock men into useful membership of society is to link their status and rewards in the wider group to their acceptance and performance of gender-defined family roles. When this connection is weakened - as for example after the French and Russian revolutions - then men's morale and behaviour deteriorates and families suffer. This is now being discovered again, and it will not be long before we will all be exhorting each other to accept men as they are, and work with the grain, and to forget ideas about how it is patriarchal culture that makes them different from women. Then, once again, they will become *more* like women.

Ch.4
FULL CIRCLE IN THE SEXUAL REVOLUTION[1]

It is generally accepted that a revolution has taken place in sexual relationships over the last twenty to thirty years, and that the conventions previously governing how these should be organised, and what personal exchanges they entail, are no longer tenable. But I believe that both the nature of this revolution and where it may be leading us are widely misunderstood.

The orthodox interpretation emphasises that medical, demographic and economic changes in the West have come together in recent decades to liberate individuals - especially women - from societal regulations which are no longer needed or wanted. In a world of smaller and later families, people can negotiate with each other to live how they like, without church or state telling them what to do.

I believe that this is only part of the story. What has been largely forgotten in public accounts is the extent to which the former regulation of relationships was rooted in the give and take occurring inside family life. The ground rules which have been discarded were not imposed on families from the public realm. They were formulated within them and were then endorsed by wider social institutions and authorities. Their removal was not really a defeat for public control, but a victory for regulation over 'private' families from the centre.

Clearly there are crucial political dimensions to this, and I suspect that contemporary libertarian orthodoxy may itself embody the

---

[1] First published in Dench 1997, and currently in print as 'Nearing full circle in the sexual revolution', in Geoff Dench (ed. 1999) *Rewriting the Sexual Contract*, New Brunswick: Transaction.

ideology of a new regime. We are still too close to events to see the links between different aspects of change in proper historical perspective. But the rise of new meritocratic elites in the West, who regarded family life as a restriction on personal freedom, must have greatly complicated the processes of adjustment by families to the new demographic possibilities. Political modernisers since the middle of the century have allied themselves with the desire of youth - all youth that is, not just the ambitious - to escape from the tiresome controls of family elders. They have also chosen lately to represent this revolution as conducted mainly by and for women. All this has been a powerful influence on directions of change.

My own recent researches (e.g. 1996b) indicate that this more critical view of 'progress', although given little space by the media, is shared by large segments of the population. The majority of ordinary people, certainly by the time they reach their mid-thirties, regret the loss of institutionalised state support for conventional family life. Many see the new state libertarianism which has replaced it not as a withdrawal of interference in private lives so much as the exercise of a new set of rules privileging a powerful interest group. This perceived new elite, which has definite 'meritocratic' features, consists of professional 'two-career' couples, who are better off when taxed as independent workers, plus a growing entourage of fellow-travelling adult 'singles' whose relative affluence is similarly promoted by fiscal policies treating 'family life' as an individual lifestyle choice. Far from allowing people to choose what is best for themselves, current state policies minimising community restraints on this group may ignore the wishes of the majority concerning the type of collective supports they would like to see provided, thereby making it harder for them to run their own families as they want.

I further suspect that the political mobilisation of anti-family sentiments over the last generation has probably delayed the adaptation of sexual divisions of labour to changing demographic circumstances. What could have been a process of pragmatic and incremental adjustment has been turned into a lengthy and conflictual sexual revolution. We will still get there, but only now that harmful consequences of the revolutionary deregulation of family life are at last being recognised. This is happening partly because such effects of change take their time to work through. But it is more the result of movement by the rebellious youth of the nineteen-sixties and seventies into grandparenthood, and adoption themselves of elder status and a managerial perspective towards family life.

At the same time, and reinforcing this, the first generation of meritocrats have taken their place within the establishment and no longer need to tear up the social fabric to create space. Indeed, among their children there is now a widespread return to tradition, with a revival of domestic service occupations and class consciousness to match the social divisions which meritocracy has itself produced, and to help them sidestep sexual labour demarcation disputes within their own households. So there is now no need to continue a social revolution which never has had a genuinely popular basis. As we move into the new millennium we can expect a steady return to normalcy in family and sexual relations.

Sexual revolution and youth culture

There are many questions raised by the argument I am putting forward, only a few of which can be dealt with here. What I want to focus on mainly is how a revolt which was originally directed against parents, then probably encouraged by a rising elite, appears to have turned into a conflict between women and men, and what the implications of this may have been.

A major misconception in the orthodox interpretation of the sexual revolution, and an important key to its ideological role, lies in its portrayal of 'traditional' social structures as serving the interests of men. Virtually all societies, and certainly all of any complexity, are 'patriarchal' in the sense of attaching greater formal rights and responsibilities to men. But as I have argued in detail elsewhere (1996a) this does not mean that these systems serve men. In most cultures it has, on the contrary, been seen as implying that the social position of men is more problematic. Men have a much greater tendency to be marginal to community life, so that in order to develop orderly motivations and have any chance of approaching the level of socialisation achieved by women they need to have their obligations and rewards spelt out and made public. Without these cultural roles, human societies would be much closer to those of other species, which revolve openly around females. Patriarchal rules and roles are instruments for mobilising men.

The notion that patriarchy and traditional society can be equated with male domination seems to be a political tool, and to become most salient during periods of intense social revolution when, I suspect, it provides a useful device for engendering support among women for the dismantling of existing institutions and undermining incumbent elites. Historically the likes of Engels and Robespierre have turned the idea of patriarchy to their own purposes, and I think that it has similarly been a key factor in the postwar attack on hereditary class structures by statist meritocracies.

The importance of having female support for a social revolution hinges on, and I think also helps to indicate, the very central position of women in society. It is women who perform the great bulk of essential work, whose relationships of mutual support form the basis of community life, and who know best how society works. They are accordingly the main guardians and transmitters of culture, with a considerable stake in existing practices and institutions. Men largely take their moral leads from women, and tend to see male activities as instrumental, executing goals defined by women. A movement which does not have some women on its side, approving its ends, will lack legitimacy and will not get very far.

Among women it is always likely to be the younger who become allies of revolutionary ideas. They are often strongly controlled by the older, and in those societies we currently regard as most patriarchal it is older people generally, not least women, who are seen explicitly by younger people as the holders of real power. Young women usually accept this authority. They need the help of older women during the long years of childcare, respect their knowledge and experience, are attached to them by family ties, and recognise their own stake in the system as future family managers. But there are tensions involved too, which can be played on by advocates of social change. If a young woman can be persuaded that the wider community will provide her with the opportunities and personal care and resources to enable her to raise her children without submission to the will and whims of a mother or mother-in-law, then she may well be prepared to endorse a programme of social transformation and impart her female licence to its cause. By weaning young women away from solidarity with older, and weakening families, revolutionaries can gain legitimacy for their centralised regimes - in which people are controlled by rewards and punishments issuing from the state - while reducing the competing authority and decentralising social influence of older people.

Such attacks on the private realm of family life are by their nature also liable to set women against men. Families run closer to women's hearts than men's, and discreetly empower women in relation to men. The devaluing of families by political revolutionaries may appeal at an intellectual level to young women. But by alienating them from family values and placing private life under greater control of the public realm in which men are visibly dominant, it sooner or later leads women to develop a sense of subordination to men, and general victimhood, which far fewer of them experience in more settled times when society and the state are according due respect to family life and motherhood.

What happened in the West during the sixties and early seventies can be seen as a classic case of the co-option of young, idealistic women as handmaidens for somebody else's social revolution. We tend to think of the sixties phenomenon as a movement by women against male oppression. But this aspect was taken on later as it became politicised. In essence the original sixties thing was a generation revolt against parents and the established 'society' they stood for. Young women were especially prominent in it from the outset. The combination of the postwar expansion of education and career opportunities with improving contraception meant that they were suddenly less dependent on families and older people, and freer to behave more like young men did. Their participation helped to make the movement socially significant and amenable to exploitation by political modernisers. But in the early years at least it was from elders and stuffy tradition that women felt liberated, not from men, who were seen as allies in the new-found freedom. It was a generalised youth culture, not feminism, which characterised the spirit of the era.

Meritocracy's female face

It was not long however before youthful revolution became overlaid with the imagery of a sex war. At first this was mainly tactical, through use of young women as symbols of modernity. But as tactics came to govern strategy, and young women started to believe in their own revolutionary destiny, eventually it became a sex war in substance as well.

The major driving force in these developments has I believe been the rising meritocracy, generated by the pace of technological changes and educational expansion, which was represented in Britain mainly in the modernising wing of the Labour Party since Harold Wilson's first administration. Wilson came to power on a wave of revulsion against Conservative cynicism and corruption, epitomised by the Profumo affair. The party was starting to lose its traditional working-class base, after opposing immigration controls, and Wilson's governing plan, which some at the time believed might keep the party in power for the rest of the century, lay in developing a new constituency among the ballooning class of upwardly-mobile technocrats.

Wilson had no problem appealing directly to women in this reconstruction of Britain, and in using them in turn as images of the future. Opening up opportunities 'to all talents' had special and genuine relevance to girls, because women were the largest untapped pool of labour. Modernising the economy was portrayed in terms of replacing sweaty old factories powered by coal and muscle with clean new science-based industries using brainpower. A New Jerusalem fit for bright young women would be built on the social ruins bequeathed by Mac's dirty old men. The old regime took on a male aspect. When coming into disagreement with their mothers many girls used this - perhaps conveniently reducing tension a bit in the process - by defining them not as the real villains but simply as 'friends of the enemy' (Mooney, 1993).

This identification of progress with womankind came to have particular importance when the social foundations for the new order were laid. Wilson's young supporters wanted to be freed from the family obligations which tied them down. Nothing is quite so irksome to a meritocrat as endless demands from relatives, and the party came under increasing pressure from younger members to promote personal freedom of choice. Certain reforms, for example those liberalising divorce and abortion, required specific legislation. Here the obvious fact that a majority of young women supported change was used to justify new laws even though the measures were widely unpopular in the country. Young women, after all, were the future. Their opinions had an over-riding legitimacy.

Other measures indirectly promoting freedom from family ties were developed under cover of executive action and Finance Bills. Wilson and then Callaghan both expanded state social services very rapidly, enabling many people to pass responsibility for the care of troublesome or burdensome relatives onto the state with a clearer conscience, and providing direct support to citizens in their own right rather than as members of families. Reforms in the structure of taxation which whittled away the financial interdependence of partners and incentives for marriage soon followed.

All this shunted a great deal of caring activity out from the private realm of family, where it hindered women's careers and had required them to be supported by male 'family wages', into the public realm where they created more congenial paid work for qualified women. Here again legitimacy had to be conjured up for this transfer. Many older women were not happy about it, but the visibly female character and staffing of the new social service professions neutralised their reservations.

These developments were profoundly altering the balance of power between female generations and their respective capacities to influence public definitions of family life and values.

Undermining older women and the private realm

Most older, traditional women were accustomed to exercising personal authority over younger members of their families. They also tended to contribute to public debate mainly through men, and considered this to be good for family life, as the resulting role for men as family spokesmen helped both to make them more responsible, and to give them a direct interest in family affairs. This double act between women and their sons and partners was to be seriously undermined by the growing participation of younger women in the public realm. For these now expected to speak for themselves, and their combination of moral legitimacy as women and eagerness to 'communicate' gave them tremendous promotional advantages over older women and men alike. Soon they started to assume that they were speaking for women as a whole, and set about redefining personal and sexual relations on terms which better suited themselves, but went outside of, or beyond, what most women desired.

Thus a transition was set in motion, some time around the middle of the seventies, whereby activist women moved from being female voices for meritocracy and began to articulate the interests of women against men. The handmaidens of revolution decided to do things for themselves. Commenting last year on Tessa Jowell's announcement of Labour plans for a Ministry for

Women, the Telegraph leader-writer noted acidly that 'Assuming that women did object to being represented by male politicians, it is difficult to think of a woman less typical than one who has become a Labour MP'.[2] But during the seventies it was precisely this type of woman who was springing up as spokesperson for the future. The femocrat was evolving. Such women were highly committed to careers and to collectivist political activity, and scornful of conventional family life. They believed that personal power via the labour market was the only sort worth having. Many were very disappointed that men, former allies in revolution, were not themselves spontaneously opting for an 'egalitarian' sharing of roles across home and work, and saw confrontation in the public realm as offering the best way of putting pressure on them.

They did not believe that traditional ways of dealing with men, within families, were relevant or effective, and had little reason to respect the life experience of older women, or even listen to them at all. So the views of older women, which could no longer be expressed usefully via men because of the growing identification of men with reaction and the oppression of women, were losing public force and value. As dissenting voices were stilled, a pattern of gender division and conflict took shape around policies seeking strict public equality of men and women.

These have enjoyed a long monopoly of legitimacy. Only as their full implications have started to unfold have sceptical voices been listened to again.

The family strikes back

In Michael Young's satirical novel (1958) the meritocracy falls to a popular revolt, led by an alliance of communitarian young women and older male socialists. In real life nothing so colourful has

---

[2] Daily Telegraph, July 2nd 1996.

happened yet, and today's Girton women seem to be the embodiment of progressive zeal rather than the counter-revolutionaries prophesied.[3]

However, there are signs that much more importance is now - or perhaps it is still - attached to the private realm than modernisers are willing to appreciate, and also that more people are starting to expect the state to help families on ordinary families' own terms.[4] Class differences may help to obscure this. People in elite positions can find personal fulfilment and satisfaction in the public realm. For most people though this sense of value comes through close personal ties with others, where family life is central.

Thus most mothers do not want to be so involved in the labour market that they cannot play a major part in bringing up their children, especially when they are young. They do not want to be herded into full-time work while their children attend full-time nurseries. Parenting is not for them just a job like any other, where all that matters is 'skill' measured according to some universalist criteria. It is a personal relationship, located very clearly within the private rather than public domain, and a key to life-long moral exchanges between generations. Above all it constitutes a major source of personal meaning and autonomy. For many women in ordinary jobs, full-time work is alienating. The best assistance that the state can provide for them as mothers lies in ensuring decent 'family wages' for men, enabling women to receive enough financial support from male partners during the child-rearing years.

---

[3] For a discussion of the gender aspects of *The Rise of the Meritocracy* see chapter 2 above.

[4] As Ferdinand Mount points out, throughout history families have repeatedly needed to fight with centralising states to retain some immunity or autonomy. We are now entering the stage in such a struggle at which a newly established political elite reluctantly starts to concede the 'strength and value' of the family. See Mount, 1982.

This judgement may seen odd; even archaic. But it is I believe true for many women. If we think otherwise then this may be because it is not the sort of interpretation which finds favour in the public realm, and so does not get widely disseminated. Popular attitudes on these matters are not reported fully and honestly, and this is in large part because media people and academic researchers are mainly modernisers, who see themselves moreover as having a missionary role. Even when very clear evidence of public indifference or hostility to radical restructuring of family lifestyles turns up, it is liable to become less convincing in their hands.

To take just one example here, it is interesting to look at how the latest report arising out of the National Child Development Study deals with its findings (in Ferri & Smith, 1996). This is a piece of 'longitudinal' research using periodic re-interviewing to chart the lives of a panel of children born during a week in 1958. The latest volume deals with panel members and their partners in 1991, at the age of 33. The main thrust of the report, which articles in the press covering the publication reflected, is that the quality of family life of respondents is dependent on the level of involvement of men. Male work, especially the time spent at it, is revealed as the enemy of happy families. The broad conclusion drawn is the sexually egalitarian one that work and family life should be shared more between men and women. Surprise, surprise.

There is of course some basis for this interpretation. Tables in the report show definite links between the amount of time spent by men at work, the general happiness of female partners, and the latters' assessment of the extent to which their men shared in family chores. However, some of their data is not very 'hard'. Thus the measures of male partners' levels of sharing in family work are rather subjective, and distinguish in a very rule-of-thumbish way between high and low involvement. It seems possible to me that women who are happy with their lives and partners will be more likely to report them as doing a decent share of housework, than will those who are not, so that the variable presented as dependent, 'happiness', may in fact have a considerable influence on the other.[5] As a result many of the correlations are circular and self-serving. But on balance a case is made for the relevance of male work in family relations.

What is wrong with the report though is that it fails to give at the same time an adequate indication of the popularity of traditional gender roles among participants in the study. Some other tabulations in the report show the connections between the level of happiness of respondents and the type of sexual division of labour in their household. The measures of sex roles used in these are technically stronger than those subjectively distinguishing between high and low male involvement. They are not based on off-the-cuff assessments, but are determined by the objective employment status of household members. So the fact that these findings are given very little prominence in the report, and are absent from press coverage, is very telling. It suggests that there is not deemed to be an audience for what they have to show.

What they do show, quite unambiguously, is that those respondents recording the highest levels of general satisfaction with life were those living in 'traditional' households. The pattern of responses on this is remarkably consistent. The highest levels of happiness, and lowest levels of unhappiness, among both men and women, are found in households where the wife is a housewife and the husband the sole earner. Similarly, the lowest levels of happiness, and highest levels of unhappiness, for men and women, are found in role reversal households where the wife works and the husband stays at home. Those with some type of 'dual career' pattern, or no earner, came in between (ibid: Table 23, page 43).

Levels of contentment are thus directly associated with mutual dependence around thoroughly conventional, sexually-specific roles. This is not explored in any detail in the report, and where

---

[5] If for no other reason than the traditional one that it shows them to have their men under proper control.

further details are given these conflict fundamentally with the report's main argument. For example, the single earner fathers are the category most likely to work long hours, which is in general terms presented as being hostile to family life. But this does not appear to stop their wives being the happiest group of female respondents! Similarly this group of households is not well placed economically, by comparison with dual earners. Thus "The fact that as many as one in three families with only the father in employment were in the bottom income quartile underlines the importance of two earned incomes for a satisfactory standard of living." (ibid.: p.16) But clearly this does not seem to matter to this category of respondents! The conclusions of the report, which focus mainly around the need for state intervention to promote more involved fathers - such as through paternity leave regulations - do not arise at all clearly out of the data collected, and seem unconcerned with its subjects' own values and perceptions.

What makes this particular study significant is that we are not dealing here with a generation of entrenched older people refusing to accept that the world is changing. The respondents were in their early thirties when interviewed. They were children during the late sixties and early seventies when new lifestyles were being pioneered. The fact that they are now choosing sexually-defined lives means that our present-day mix of lifestyle prescriptions cannot seriously be portrayed as a transitional stage on the road to strict equality. This, perhaps, is the simple truth which is too unpalatable to be spelt out.

This example also indicates the insidious consequences of allowing our ideas about family life to be controlled within the public realm, where professionals and modernisers occupy most powerful positions. Those young people found to be happy in their traditional lives are not getting any feed-back endorsing their lifestyle choices. In fact the main public messages arising out of the study they participated in could well suggest to them that they are deviants, or part of a dwindling and doomed minority. No wonder that young people are said to be confused.

I suspect that many people's personal experiences, especially women's, are in conflict with what they read about family life in the press. But the longer that they live their own experiences, and come to trust their own feelings, the more chance they have of developing a healthy scepticism towards orthodox accounts. So it is among older women, not the girls of Girton, that opposition to sexual revolution attacking conventional families, and an explicit rediscovery of the importance of the private realm, has been gradually building up.

My own research findings (1996b) show that as they grow older, moving through the life-cycle and seeing the consequences of sexual revolution from different perspectives, many women become seriously concerned about the future of families in Britain under current social policies. They worry about idle and feckless adult sons who seem to have no stake in society, about daughters who cannot find reliable and committed partners to help raise their children, and about grandchildren denied the security of a stable home-life and from whom they may even be alienated by relationship problems or breakdown in the parental generation. And many blame 'alternative' family conventions for spawning all of these problems.

The women who resisted parental pressures and threw off convention in the sixties and seventies have moved into authoritative positions, as grandmothers, in the private realm. Few might want to restore the patterns of family life of the fifties in their entirety. But most now believe in broadly conventional sexual partnerships - entailing long-term mutual commitment and some sexual differentiation of roles - as the basis for successful rearing of children. They are a force to be respected. Having stood against their parents in the sixties and seventies, this generation of women is not going to put up with younger women, or governments citing only them, telling them what to do. The counter-revolutionaries are the original rebels themselves, grown older and wiser.

Repairing the damage of revolution

The wheel of sexual revolution is turning, and we are collectively rediscovering that conventional families and roles may offer after all the surest basis for community life, and above all for rearing children. Whereas in the eighties and early nineties almost the only popular articles about family life, outside of the Daily Mail, were phrased in terms of the importance of defending (women's) choice, there is now a fuller diet of views available in most papers on what may be happening to family life and on possible links between changes in sexual partnerships and wider developments in society like the gap between work-rich and work-poor classes. The concerns of the private realm are breaking through into the public.

But that does not mean we can just go back to how things used to be, even if we wanted to. The world has moved on and objective technological and demographic changes mean that a revitalised family will have to reflect new realities. This certainly means a larger direct role for women, freed from much domestic drudgery, in the public realm. It may also, to a lesser extent, mean a larger domestic role for men. I am not greatly impressed by many of the claims that men are already doing more, as these are too often based on the notion that historically they did nothing. Here again the National Child Development Study has some fascinating but under-publicised findings. For example, the fathers of panel-members in the early nineteen-sixties survey, before these issues had become politicised, seem to have done marginally more childcare and housework than reported for their sons in 1992, when there were large prizes of moral virtue to be earned in the public realm by declaring it (Ferri & Smith: pp. 30/31). So things may have changed less than we think, or in different ways. By the same token, altering people's behaviour, that is men's, may be achieved more easily by operating within the context of traditional sex-specific roles, than through divisive public sex war.

Where the sexual revolution may actually have the most lasting consequences seems likely to be where it started - that is in generation terms. Development of young adult lifestyles which do not revolve around the care of children has effectively created a new life stage of liberated adulthood, which can be enjoyed before responsible parenthood for most people or, for those adults who choose not to have children at all, offer an alternative to conventional family life. This new or enlarged stage in the life cycle can accommodate a variety of new lifestyles in which very different forms of sexual contract, or even no contract at all, can apply. We now have a burgeoning singles culture, which has evolved out of sixties innovation and experimentation and caters for many adults, including homosexuals, who want to opt out of family life altogether. It has transformed city centres and people's lifestyle options, and there is every reason to believe that with longer life-spans these choices will continue to evolve and multiply.

It is one thing to welcome a flowering of adult lifestyle choices. It is quite another to regard these as providing appropriate settings for bringing up children; and something which does emerge very clearly from my own research is that most people with experience of childrearing believe that in households with children conventional family patterns are best, and that these need support and encouragement in the community which they do not at present get. As the example of many non-European cultures shows, it is fine to have 'free' states for adults who are just looking after themselves. But once they have children dependent on them then it is better to live in conventional family systems, where people have consistent and compatible expectations of mutual care and support.

Where we have perhaps made a mistake in Britain over the last twenty to thirty years, or rather our political masters have on our behalf, is in seeing alternatives to conventional families as morally equal to them. Families built around agreed mutual expectations are fundamental to social and community life in ways that these alternatives are not. They provide a stable environment for rearing the next generation. They set a framework of key personal relationships, with people of all sex and age categories, which endure when other ties may fade, and which provide the context for practising give and take and learning about fundamental social behaviour and values. They give us a place in what would otherwise be an anomic universe. Without a menu of lifestyle options we could survive. Without family life communities would soon disintegrate.

The lesson we must re-learn is that a sound polity has to be built around respect for the autonomy and priority of the private realm. What this means in practice is the state restoring a privileged position to families rather than taxing them as a form of individual consumption. And it also means restoring power to parents against the experts and professionals in the public realm, like teachers and social workers, who have increasingly seen it as their public duty to interfere in family life and tell or advise parents what to do. Most parents do not want to be taught what to do - increasingly, it has to be said, by people with academic qualifications but no personal experience of parenting themselves - but want simply to be allowed to get on with it. Very many people cannot understand how and why this is no longer the case.

This is arguably the single most important factor behind current alienation of ordinary people from politicians, and there is an interesting test ahead for the Labour Party, which still appears to be programmed to pursue strict gender symmetry rather than the needs of whole families. Ironic as it may seem in the light of Labour Party performance and its closeness to the modernising movement, many older women appear to have voted Labour in 1997 in despair at the continuing failure of the Conservatives to come up with measures to match their pro-family rhetoric. The Children Act addressed some obvious problems, and the Child Support Agency looked to have the right objectives. But little had been done to revive tax incentives for marriage, or to back up the rights of parents against intrusive professionals, or tackle the roots of family poverty.

Although the signs so far are not encouraging, New Labour may do better than this. By getting so many women into parliament it has in an important sense already dealt with the symbolic business of gender parity. Now it can turn to matters of substance. When it does so it will discover what ordinary women really want, and might respond to this because of the electoral consequences.

Older women are a large and growing sector of the electorate. In 1992 they kept the Conservatives in power against pollsters' predictions. Most are by inclination more in tune with Tory world-views, and this more than anything probably accounts for Labour's long exile in the wilderness. If Labour is to have any hope of keeping their vote at the next election it will need to re-examine its attitude in government towards the private realm. This is perhaps the most potent reason for believing that this cycle of revolution is nearly complete.

Ch.5
MEN, FAMILIES AND CAREERS[1]

The idea of a career bears some connotations which are very often glossed over in contemporary analyses of work. I suspect that this is because they draw our attention towards several crucial differences between the social context and meaning of work for men and women, which many commentators would prefer to avoid. There are important issues involved here which should however be confronted, and which I think are now becoming admissible topics of debate again. I intend to go with that trend here.

What distinguishes a career from (mere) work is the decisiveness and strength of its location in the public realm. Work or labour in a broad sense can embrace activities undertaken purely to keep together one's body and soul, and those of one's family members, and which, as in subsistence or peasant economies, may impinge very little on wider social and economic structures. By contrast a career cannot exist without these wider frameworks. It is precisely through their elaboration and refinement as spheres of endeavour which are separate from family networks that such structures provide opportunities for the development of a career orientation.

Through a career, an individual is enabled to make a direct contribution to a community purpose which goes beyond that of a particular family group. A career is universalistic, and follows impersonal criteria and rules which make it open to all who are prepared to subordinate themselves to its imperatives and commit themselves to its objectives. As such, a career is inherently

---

[1] Published in 1997 under this title in Yochanan Altman (ed) *Careers in the New Millennium*, Leuven/Amersfoort: Acco.

competitive, offering personal fulfilment and rewards commensurate with success in serving explicit goals and, by implication, in detaching from personal relationships which conflict with or distract from universalist endeavours.

This brings us to the core feature of a career, for my present purpose, which is that it generates a licence to neglect the performance of interpersonal obligations in the 'private' realm of family relationships. Deflect may be a better word here than neglect. The social institutions within which careers are pursued usually recognise the importance of family life, and may at some level (as in national ideologies, corporate mission statements and so on) explicitly acknowledge the fundamental and ultimately sovereign character of family ties. But for the public realm to operate efficiently, it needs to have a call on people occupied within it which routinely overrides the demands of families, and for operational purposes requires them to ignore these demands or, where the duties are pressing, to organise substitution or delegation whereby someone else performs them on their behalf. A worker in the public realm who is not willing or able to accord this level of priority to the job cannot properly refer to their engagement as a career.

It is this aspect of a career which, in the discourse of equal opportunities, renders the conventional organisation of work discriminatory against women. But I would argue that this is to look at things too negatively. It is also possible, and in the longer run more valuable, to see it as embodying very clearly how and why careers are particularly important to men. For they offer a particularly efficient way, and I would suggest socially productive, of involving men in useful social activity. There is not the space here to develop my case in detail, so I shall just concentrate on a few salient points. (A much fuller presentation of this argument can be found in Dench 1996a.)

The essence of my argument is that, notwithstanding the imagery of patriarchy, men are in reality very marginal in most societies, which revolve essentially around families and interpersonal relations, in which women always play a central part. The motivations arising out of family life are fundamentally important in providing incentives for orderly participation in all societies, including our own, and men are liable to be drones unless they are co-opted to family groups. As they cannot compete with women when it comes to affective relations, and on the whole do not want to, they are most readily incorporated as performers of instrumental tasks. So the notion of a career, in which it is possible to work hard on behalf of or in the name of a family but without getting too involved in it, and without being seen as disloyal or hypocritical for failing to become closely involved in it emotionally, represents a valuable cultural device for maximising the input of men to communities. The career stands as a neat metaphor to conjure up specifically male commitment to family life. As we move into a new millennium there seems now to be a rediscovery taking place of this sort of sexual difference, and a readiness to confront it rather than deny or run away from it.

The centrality of family

The idea of a career is important for men principally because female domination of family and interpersonal relations always has been, and probably always will be, fundamental to community life and to women's power in society. Even where men appear to be controlling families, this usually contains large elements of what I have called the 'theatre of patriarchy', whereby men are playing roles and upholding rules which may give them some individual authority or personal status but which serve women's interests more systematically. The notion of career, as prestigious work and destiny in another realm, provides a countervailing source of value which is especially important for men and thereby for securing men's involvement in families. What makes it so useful is not just that it is consistent with a degree of male detachment from the intimacies of family life but that it also, very significantly, manages to redefine this as a special form of contribution. This helps men to negotiate a role in families which is complementary to that of women, rather than competing with women or being too obviously subordinate.

The central place of women in human communities is irreducible and arises out of their role in the organisation of reproduction, which is at the heart of social life. Men everywhere, as indeed males in most species, are inclined towards being social outsiders. Their usefulness to groups varies much more than women's, and depends greatly on the way in which social institutions define and reward their roles. Women in all societies are more responsive to each other's needs, and to the value of a social contract. In the last analysis, this is because they know they need society more. The long and arduous process of child-rearing makes women become interdependent and value co-operation with others in a way which does not so readily apply to men, who can more easily get along by themselves and - when society permits it - avoid responsibilities towards others. Society is at heart female, and is built around shared motherhood.

In all 'traditional' cultures there is a more or less explicit awareness of this centrality of motherhood, and of the need to create distinctive roles for men in order to give them a comparable stake in society. We all need to feel needed by others, if we are to learn to be responsive to them. Unless adult men are given clear roles and duties their attachment to society is very tenuous.

The explicit highlighting of male roles which results, and corresponds broadly to what we call patriarchy, has two main aspects. Firstly, men are made socially responsible for the support of particular women and children, usually but not necessarily their sexual partners and own (presumed or acknowledged) offspring. This makes men more like women, by giving them specific people to care about in the way that mothers have to care for their children. Secondly, they are given formal rights and duties, usually linked to a 'head of family' status, in public structures of political and economic institutions used for organising access to the means of support. This representative role increases their opportunity and hence their motivation to carry out obligations to their families.

As David Gilmore's cross-cultural study of men shows (1990), in the small handful of cultures without patriarchy men live a narcissistic Peter Pan existence, putting very little into the community and leaving virtually all labour to women. Such societies have not developed beyond a rudimentary level, and cannot compete with more highly organised and structured neighbours. This is why there are so few of them. They are not a suitable model for modern industrial nations to copy; though that has not stopped us from trying.

By-passing men

I have suggested elsewhere that historically the impetus towards patriarchal conventions has come basically from women, concerned to get men to play a more useful role in society and be more responsible for the wellbeing of others (1996a, chapter 5). If this is the case though it has lately been forgotten, as many modern women see men's family roles less as the source of greater equality than as instruments for male domination. Since the Enlightenment the philosophical doctrines of individualism have come into repeated conflict with ideas about sexual differences. During this century, as states have become willing to channel increasingly direct supports to women, some libertarians, especially in Protestant countries, have portrayed male family roles as a major source of social evil.

This characterisation has led to rejection of men's specific economic role as the main provider and source of family income. Eleanor Rathbone, for example, persuaded parliament in 1945 to by-pass husbands and pay family allowances direct to mothers, after conducting a long campaign against what she dubbed the 'Turk complex'.

> It is easy to see what satisfaction the institution of the dependent family gives to all sorts and conditions of men - to the tyrannous man what opportunities of tyranny, to the selfish of self-

> indulgence, to the generous of preening himself in the sunshine of his own generosity, to the chivalrous of feeling himself the protector of the weak. ... Thus when a proposal *(for direct state support of women)* presents itself which is obnoxious to the hidden Turk in man, he stretches up his hand from his dwelling in the unconscious mind and the proposal disappears from the upper regions of consciousness. (1924: p.270-1)

Rathbone herself was mainly concerned with improving the status of motherhood, by defining it as a public role deserving state support in its own right. But her breach of the boundary between private and public realms, and dismissal of male family motivations (but not of female) as rooted in an 'instinct of domination', contributed to a de-legitimising of distinctive male family roles. It was a factor in the emergence of a new statist political economy in which segregated roles are deemed harmful to society and where men who still aspire to them are regarded as morally deviant or pathetic throw-backs.

This process has become intensified since the sixties, when the emergence of the pill, allowing much more reliable planning of families, encouraged women to start claiming equal participation in the formerly male-oriented public realm. This development has helped to weaken further the framework of family responsibilities which previously underpinned men's motivation to take on socially useful labour. Some of this is revealed in Neil Lyndon's retrospective baring of soul:

> If we didn't have to have babies when we had regular sex, it followed that we didn't have to get married. And if we didn't have to support families, we didn't have to have jobs or careers: and if we didn't have to have careers, ... what might we not do? Or be? A *tabula rasa* of adult masculinity had been presented to us, upon

which we might (we supposed) make our marks
as we pleased. (1992: p.96-7)

Family ties may not be important for men in the same ways that they are for women. But they are I believe nevertheless crucial for them, and in particular for men's development of incentives to participate fully in orderly social life. I suspect that dismantling of the idea that a career is particularly significant for a man, and that families need men to aspire to careers, may be having profoundly negative consequences for societies at large. For although often linked to the drive towards a greater sharing of tasks between men and women, the rejection of 'mainly male' careers may, paradoxically, have led to a collapse not only in male participation in public realm activities themselves, but also to their involvement in family work in the private realm too. The pursuit of strict equality between men and women in career aspirations may be counterproductive. Far from leading to a more equitable sharing of roles, it could be piling ever greater burdens on women.

The pursuit of gender symmetry

My suspicions here arise out of research which I have been carrying out over several years, and which was reported last year (Dench, 1996b). The findings indicate how our growing failure in the West to acknowledge the importance of family obligations in providing basic life motivations to men may now be seriously weakening their productive contribution to modern social life. In my main study I found that most women expect to have dependents, and that this gives them reasons to participate fully in society and develop a place in the community. But the same no longer seems so true of men. Many now feel that women do not want 'dependence', and that families and the community in general can manage without men. This leaves many without a role, and with little incentive to become responsive members of the community.

We have failed to anticipate this problem, I think, because in an age of individualism we overlook that being needed by other people is essential to the development of responsible adult status in society, and that this is not and perhaps never can be available to men on the same basis as women. Social changes pursued in ignorance of this mean that this socialising experience is being lost for a growing proportion of men. In less individualistic societies and families there was a sense of interdependence which gave everyone a valued place. But the deregulation of family life in the West has weakened this, certainly for men, so that the fundamental lack of symmetry in the positions of men and women, which patriarchy helped to overcome and to obscure, is starting to be exposed again. By attacking sexual divisions of labour, on the assumption that gender differences are artificial and malleable, we may actually be causing further polarisation rather than the desired harmonisation of men's and women's life experiences.

Women in all societies, through their direct responsibility for children, are more alert to the importance of interdependence and have much easier access to a sense of being needed. In patriarchal family systems men become pulled in too. But this does not occur so easily in the more libertarian family patterns which are now emerging. Women have not had responsibility for children taken away from them, and still have this as a source of meaning and personal motivation - at the same as enjoying greater opportunities themselves for participation in the public domain and pursuit of careers.

For men the opposite applies. New family values emphasising personal choice do not actually exclude men from family life. But they specify that family roles are optional, and in particular argue against blind acceptance of the traditional convention that men should support families. This makes it easier for men themselves to avoid family obligations, for women to decide to manage without them, and for couples to split when the hassle of 'negotiating' sexual roles becomes too tedious. As a result it is mainly men who get left out of families, and whose sense of purpose - and corresponding ability to cope with pressures and obstacles outside of the family as well as inside - may become seriously diminished.

I would argue therefore that the difficulties which many men are now experiencing in the public realm may have arisen, paradoxically again perhaps, because we have failed to see or chosen to ignore that the main personal motivations for most people - even 'career' motivations ostensibly focused very explicitly outside of family life - are generated within the private domain. And in order to tackle the problems now emerging we will have to appreciate the corollary, that the public realm of work is itself perhaps less of a key to social life and personal motivations than we have come to suppose.

We often hear the argument that contemporary male demoralisation results from long term unemployment. But purely economic trends fail to explain adequately what has happened to men in recent decades. There have been many periods of high male unemployment in the past; but during them men's interest in work, and readiness to retrain themselves for new opportunities, has been enhanced. This no longer seems the case for many men in Britain, and the reason for this change seems to be that family roles and expectations made of men have altered. Men are told all the time - through newspapers and the television if not face to face within families - that women want to be independent and to do things for themselves. So whereas there used to be altruistic incentives for men to compete and succeed at work, and which boys anticipated at school, there are now altruistic reasons instead (not to mention welfare back-ups) for standing aside to let women do things for themselves. Whereas male ambition may be sharpened by competition among men to serve women, and to support families, it seems to be weakened by the rhetoric of female independence.

Several of the respondents in my recent studies have been men who had become unemployed following the stress of the break-up of a marriage or relationship - itself often precipitated by domestic disagreements over the family provider role. What was very significant was that many of the men who accepted the idea of fully equal opportunities seemed to slip quite quickly into apathy and idleness. But those who told themselves that their partners were making a mistake, and might change their minds, or who felt that their children still needed support from their father too, showed much greater resolve in getting back into work. As George Gilder showed with such verve (1973), what happens in families is fundamentally important to the health of the economy.

The chimera of equal careers

It is commonly argued that, given a little time and a bit of a shove or encouragement, men will develop orientations towards work and family which are identical with those women, and that some indeed already have done so. Moves for symmetrical parental leave entitlements or flexible work practices are frequently prefaced with assertions that this is the way that things are now moving, and that men either do now, or soon will, want this. The evidence I have seen though is far from conclusive proof of a movement towards a world of gender equality.

Adrienne Burgess for example (1997; plus Burgess & Ruxton 1996) refers to numbers of men seeking more equitable divisions of caring and paid work with their partners, and claiming to be doing more themselves in the home and as parents than men used to. At first sight her materials look fairly convincing, but the experience of doing research myself in this area makes me sceptical about her analysis and conclusions. To start with the actual changes imputed to men's behaviour, here as in many other studies, bear no comparison with the significance attached to them. Insofar as figures are given, most of the men who are 'doing more' in the home and as parents are still doing far less than their partners, and this fact deserves more emphasis! It is not good enough to say that we are still in a 'transitional' stage of gender-role changes, as if arrival in a promised land were guaranteed.

However, what is potentially of far greater significance, and in some ways much harder to keep an eye on, is the way in which research findings are modelled together into hypotheses and explanations. There is a considerable risk of ecological fallacies here, whereby trends which are occurring at the same time are assumed to be part of the same process. In the area of family-work transitions there are several different indicators of change which analysts frequently treat as co-variables but which more intensive research, of the sort I favour myself, may reveal as representing contrary indications. My own research findings have made me extremely cautious about how to fit together the various types of data which are being generated in this area. Hidden paradoxes, concealing hypocrisy and self-deception, abound.

Thus Burgess (like most other researchers) rather takes it for granted that the men who are doing a greater share of domestic work are the same men who believe in identical gender roles. But it may be misleading to assume that attitudes and behaviour are consistent in this way. It is an easy assumption; but is it valid? Before doing my own, more ethnographic, work on the subject I would have assumed that it was. Probably I would not have even asked myself the question. But the value of research is that it sometimes comes up with a few surprises. And my own study certainly provided some in this respect. For in it we found that those men who actually spent most time doing domestic work (though remember, of course, that this was rarely very much) tended to be men who had fairly traditional ideas about sexual divisions of labour. They put their own careers first, and saw these as the economic mainstay and foundation for the family. Having fulfilled this traditional role, they were then happy to spend some time in the kitchen, so that their partners could pursue a career too. But they did not see this as an equal career, undertaken for the family. They saw their partner's job more as providing them with emotional pin-money: something to give them an interest outside of the home and keep them happy. 'Her career' was sometimes almost like something that the man had himself provided (through his 'support') for his partner, rather than something which she was doing for him and the family; a modern 'trophy' rather than a genuine 'dual career'.

In most of these cases we came across it was clear that the man would not have been supportive towards his wife or partner's career if he had not (already) achieved a level of success within his own. This success, frequently important in furnishing the basic family income, gave him the confidence to take on domestic work as well. Such men sometimes stated explicitly that the family would not be where it was if he had not been successful in his career. He could clearly manage. Also, though this was not spelt out too explicitly, his (provenly useful) commitment to his career meant that he could withdraw legitimately from domestic involvement if it threatened to reach a level of discomfort. Because he had a career, his domestic labour liability was limited. Without that protection he might well have not been prepared to take so much on in the first place.

This type of new man behaviour is not far away from old chivalry, and surely should not be used as evidence of a shift towards interchangeability of roles for men and women. It would make more sense I think to use it to show that there is some flexibility within conventional sexual divisions of labour, and that behaviour may be easier to change, and even more important, than attitudes.

The point of this becomes even more obvious when we look at those men in my study who did appear to accept without qualification the ideology of equal opportunities and the economic importance of women's work, and were willing to contemplate the prospect of equal careers for women. For many of these proved to have opted out of domestic labour altogether. Most of them lived alone, and where they had children it was as absent fathers. Many were long-term unemployed - the antithesis of 'career-man' - and did not make even financial contributions to family life. For such men the independence of women meant that men no longer had to bother to submit to the regimes of family duty. Their willingness to join the new androgynous generation, and to reject conventional sexual roles and divisions, does not indicate a victory for equality. It suggests to me a massive and growing social imbalance whereby men are withdrawing from family and community involvement to play (or sometimes to sulk) by themselves.

Thus the apparent and widely-celebrated pursuit of egalitarian sex roles by men may be associated in practice not with new harmony and equality so much as with a growing polarisation between the lives and lifestyles of men and women. This involves a liberation of men from family duties and domestic drudgery and also from much of the incentive to pursue a career. For women it means a corresponding over-burdening with greater responsibilities, both at home and at work, together with related difficulties in finding a good balance between family and work - or perhaps also with experience of some pressure to adopt a so-called 'male' style career which for a woman may entail remaining childless.

There appears to be a basic asymmetry here between men's and women's lives and experience, which many policies designed to help women pursue careers may be aggravating rather than reducing. For men, having a career can be seen as complementary with being a family man and enjoying a broadly-based lifestyle, while for women the notion of career, with its usual implication of placing priority in the public realm, stands inherently in greater tension with the demands of family life. Thus for most women a career, as opposed to mere work, is only a feasible option where a job is so highly paid that ample domestic help can be bought in, and/or where her partner already has a manifestly successful career. For a man on the other hand having no career or career prospect may well mean not really having a place in the community, and little real value as a domestic partner.

African-Caribbeans in the vanguard.

The sort of sexual polarisation which may be promoted by neglect of the crucial nature of male careers seems to have proceeded furthest in the UK among the British African-Caribbean (A-C) community. This group was strongly represented in my recent study - and this was partly because I had been drawn in the first place into exploring links between family and work as a result of an earlier study among them (Dench, 1992). The development of gender conflicts within this community is usually seen as an outcome of their historical experience of slavery. My own analysis suggests that what is going on in Britain may have more to do with the specific encouragement among them in UK of female careers and 'independence', often (it has to be noted) by libertarian social workers who regarded themselves as promoting Caribbean lifestyles. These influences on them arise from forces in current British society. So if we want to see where present trends and policies in British family culture may be leading we may, I suggest, have something to learn from their example.

More than half of the informants in my study were drawn from minority communities, and just over one third of these (forty six individual respondents, plus the membership of several discussion groups) were of A-C origin or descent. Whereas most minority respondents held very traditional views on family life, among the A-C group there proved to be even stronger rejection of traditional sexual divisions of labour than found among white Britons. This pattern of response was linked moreover with an even greater marginalisation of men, manifested in the lowest rates of marriage and highest incidence of reported sexual conflict and sexual polarisation, with a high rate of households based on lone adults (43%), in which men appeared more apathetic, unproductive (47% men unemployed) and generally peripheral to community affairs.

Contrary to popular speculation among whites, this was however not seen as a good situation by most women in the community. While often welcoming some independence many A-C women reported themselves as having now become over-burdened by multiple demands of work, children and other family and community commitments. The group as a whole has become extremely concerned at the collapse of traditional family life, which is now a major focus of debate within it. There is a growing awareness that in promoting 'female independence' and careers among them UK social services may have been projecting an alien (i.e. UK libertarian) cultural system onto the community (James-Fergus, 1997).

This is a situation which is still seriously misunderstood by most white British people, who tend to assume that the way this minority group lives is based on its own imported cultural heritage. However the values and lifestyle now popularly identified with this community do seem to be rooted in British culture, as they are held mainly by those who have grown up here. The A-C respondents who were born in the Caribbean displayed traditional values and behaviour. Their levels of support for conventional families, male careers and 'providing', female 'caring', respect for elders and family-based supports for relatives in need, all proved greater, age for age, than those of members of the white British community. By contrast the rejection of those values and the adoption of 'alternative' lifestyles by younger group members was the strongest of any category of respondents. Among UK-born A-C respondents the rate of lone-adult households was 56% (compared with 22% of those born in the Caribbean, 18% of other minority group members, and 25% of white British).

The study found a broad difference of orientation to family life among all respondents on the basis of age. Those under 35 favoured personal choice and alternative families while those older, especially those with practical experience of managing families, supported traditional set-ups and sexual divisions. But this overall generation gap was a veritable gulf in the case of A-C respondents, with migrants and their children born here leading highly divergent lives, and often barely able to communicate with each other. Thus the lifestyle of younger African-Caribbeans does seem to be a measure of their wholesale integration to UK society. Having acculturated so rapidly and enthusiastically to the libertarian culture dominant here as they grew up, younger members of the community now find themselves acting out its implications ahead of the rest of us, and perhaps giving us an advance warning of the dangers inherent in it.

Rediscovering sexual difference and divisions

Within the African-Caribbean community a rapid and extreme polarisation between men and women seems to have occurred from the 1970s onwards, and is now being followed by urgent debate and action to restore family relationships and heal the community. In the white British majority there has I imagine been a longer and slower transformation of family culture. But here too there are signs of a turning back towards more conventional families organised around some sexual division of labour. This emerges quite strongly from my own work, which shows that in spite of great public emphasis on the radical dismantling of traditional sex roles, most people do seem to be looking for rather small changes in the behaviour of people around them. They want more flexible divisions of labour. But the majority of them, including most women - and not least many who were themselves hostile to conventional families when they were younger - seek this within a framework of 'neo-conventional' relationships, that is where there is still a broad assumption that women have primary responsibility for managing family life, while men have greater overall commitment to economic activities and a career. This is especially the case among older women. From their mid-thirties onwards women change their attitudes very definitely and consistently, with a clear movement towards a greater valuation of family life and satisfaction with the role of family manager.

I have not come across much other research which explicitly leads to similar conclusions. But this may be, as I discuss elsewhere (Dench, 1997) because many researchers and journalists are still looking and hoping for a gender-role revolution, and this influences their presentation of results. Thus the latest publication arising out of the National Child Development Study (Ferri & Smith, 1996) organises its data around the argument that mothers are more content and families get along most smoothly where fathers limit the amount of time they spend out at work and find a reasonable amount of time for sharing in family activities. Buried deeply within the report though there are a couple of tables which indicate that some of the findings, possibly the most significant, have been largely ignored.

These tables show that those respondents recording the highest levels of both personal and marital satisfaction were those living in 'traditional' families. The pattern of responses on this is remarkably consistent. In families where one or more partner is working, the highest levels of happiness, and lowest levels of unhappiness, among both men and women, are found in households where the wife is a housewife and the husband a traditional earner. Similarly, the lowest levels of happiness, and highest levels of unhappiness, for men and women, are found in role reversal households where the wife works and husband stays at home. Levels of contentment are thus directly associated with mutual dependence around conventional and sexually-specific roles. What is moreover particularly important about this study is that we are not dealing here with a generation of entrenched older people refusing to accept that the world is changing. The respondents were all aged 33 in 1992 when interviewed. They were children in the late sixties and seventies when new lifestyles were being pioneered. The fact that they are now living conventional lives means that the present mix of lifestyle prescriptions cannot really be portrayed as an ongoing transformation. What we are more likely to be in the middle of is a restoration of fairly traditional family life. Commentators are just a bit slow in noticing it.

More researchers on family and work are however coming to see not only that strict gender equality is not what most women want, but also that even where statist elites have tried to pretend that it is, the preferences of ordinary people for families built around sexual divisions of labour do prevail in the long run (Hakim, 1997). It may be difficult for us now to envisage a society (again) in which careers are openly seen as pertaining more to male than female destiny. But this does seem to be the direction in which we are moving. Patterns of life have been radically altered by medical advances, which make smaller, later families the norm. Women - especially young women before having children, and also those women of all ages who do not have children - will be able to play a much more direct part in the public realm than was possible in previous generations. But sex remains the basis of important differences in social orientation. The private realm of 'community' life will surely continue to be mainly the province of women. And those who will most need careers, and will attach most importance to them, will go on being men.

Ch.6
FATHERS, HOLY FATHERS AND THE SPIRITUAL DIMENSION[1]

During the last century the state in western societies took over and developed many of the roles formerly played by churches in providing social security and organising supports for family life. The expansion of citizenship this entailed has produced many improvements in our lives, in particular around healthcare and the provision of material security. What remains less clear is whether that sort of progress can be matched by viable interventions in family life and personal relationships. I would suggest that state action in these areas may not achieve its professed aims unless greater partnership is sought with religious or 'faith-based' groups, whose continuing pertinence we neglect at our peril. The deepening concern in Britain over fatherhood is very germane here. This issue is ideally placed to illuminate the social relevance of religion, and test the limits of state intervention carried out in isolation from such other forms of social power and organisation.

Churches and family life

In Britain many of us have forgotten just how close is the affinity between organised religion and the conduct of family life. When we talk about religion in Britain these days it is usually to condemn blind fundamentalism, stubborn conflict between entrenched communities, or wrongheaded resistance to 'progress'. This is however about religion seen from the outside, as a marker of some collective identity or solidarity. What we fail to note is that from inside religions operate largely as an extension of family

---

[1] Written for inclusion in 1999 conference report *Fathers in the New Millennium*, to be published by Family Policy Studies Centre.

life. And it is this aspect which gives them real force and popular legitimacy, and explains their durability.

In all cultures religious ideas and practices are linked with people's struggles to protect their family life against the depredations of uncaring Nature. Beliefs in immortality and souls merge easily into folk conceptions of families as ongoing chains of kin stringing their way through time, caring for each other as and when they can, living and dead, and experiencing a sort of unity in eternity. At all important points in the unfolding of a family, religion has a part to play. Management of conception and fertility are basic concerns eliciting religious thoughts and behaviour, and the selection of suitable reproductive partners typically takes place within religious communities sharing common values. Key life-course events such as marriage, birthing ceremonies and funerals are all ritualised within a religious context.

As far as we can tell this is true within all human societies, from barely-understood pre-history to the present day. Even within an advanced modern society like Britain, where few people have any time for theology, religious institutions until recently still offered the moral and conceptual frameworks within which most people - including some sceptics hedging their bets or just swimming with the tide - acted out their family lives. Affinity works both ways. It was the sharing within a church of prayers for the wellbeing of each others' family members which helped to bind communities into mutually supportive networks.

Shaping the male spirit

More specifically than this, religions provide powerful ideological props for what is potentially a weak component in any family system - and the subject of our growing concern today - which is the involvement of adult males as 'fathers'. Many cultures define the male contribution to reproduction as spiritual more than biological - balancing the clearly dominant biological role of mothers and perhaps reflecting the more explicit act of will required in fathers' commitment. Monotheistic religions give this element even greater prominence, and seem almost entirely oriented towards male responsibility for families.

Thus the concept of fatherhood is central to Christianity. God himself is the Father of everything. He is creator of the universe and responsible for its maintenance. His agents on earth, tending His people, are priests who are frequently addressed as father. And the most important role offered to ordinary men, giving them status as full members of the community, is as fathers in families for which - within God's will - they are responsible and to which they must be wholly committed.

This patriarchal feature of Christianity is often cited as evidence that it promotes male domination of women. This interpretation may be valid in some formal respects. But it overlooks a crucial paradox concerning the male character of God himself, which is that essential characteristics attributed to Him are not qualities often found among actual men. All-seeing. Ever-vigilant. Eternally-patient. All-caring. Insofar as these terms reflect ordinary mortals at all it is women who come to mind, especially mothers. God is not male in a conventional sense. What His image does conjure up is the sort of man that most women would like to have in their families as their fathers, husbands and sons; men who are strong and can hold their own among other men, but who are also caring and responsive and can be called on and relied on in the way that other women can.

Belief in a caring, male divinity is in effect exhortatory. In practical terms it sets a standard of masculinity which can help to domesticate men. Through contemplating this idealised image of man, they may come to believe that this is their own true nature, and God's will for them. This is surely why religion focuses so much attention on men. It is not because they are already made in God's image. It is more that men are the ones who need to strive most consciously and conscientiously to approach it. Women need less guidance. Because of the nature of their reproductive role and strategy they are more likely to value family life anyway. The idea of a caring male deity helps pull men too into the holy mysteries of family life, by creating a set of exemplary images and motivations which socialises them into identifying with families' needs and becoming amenable to their demands.

What is crucial here is the way in which this religious idiom encompasses the duality of male identity. It takes as given the rude, rough clay in which men are born. But it also has a vision of how they may be transformed. This elastic view of male nature gives men the confidence to believe that however implausible it may seem they can achieve orderly lives. By fashioning themselves in their maker's image, they can earn approval from their parents, their fellow-men, and the women who will enable them to become fathers in the flesh. The spirit of God which they cultivate inside themselves is a template both for redemption and for finding a constructive role in the community.

A weakening spell

This transformative process is losing force as religion plays ever less part in our lives, while the state does more. Nowhere is this more evident than in Britain. Compared with other western states, and significantly unlike the north American and Scandinavian countries which political modernisers hold up to us as examples, Britain is becoming a society in which state family policies can no longer build on a foundation of popular religious sentiment. We are reaching a point where it is I believe necessary to give serious attention to this spiritual dimension and the part it can play.

It seem very likely that research on this subject would find an association between the weakening of moral props for fatherhood generated by religion and the disappearance of men from responsible family roles. Family life in Britain is increasingly female. We have the highest rates for men living alone and single motherhood - and especially for lone teenage mothers. Meanwhile there is a flourishing 'yob culture' (or, more accurately, absence of culture) among men. This is indifferent to family life and values, and indeed to community life in general, and feeds instead a rise in anti-social behaviour and a ballooning prison population.

Official wisdom blames unemployment for this trend. But high unemployment in the past, as in the thirties when Fatherhood was still valued, produced none of it. Another explanation commonly put forward is that women do not want to be 'dependent' on men, and growth of their own rights as citizens has allowed them to shift away from reliance on patriarchal families. Obviously there is something in this. State supports have altered the context within which marriages or partnerships between men and women are negotiated. There is a new dialogue and dialectic, in which women may feel that they should expect a greater display of caring and commitment from a man before cementing any relationship. This rarely amounts to a desire for independence, though: more a bid for emotional closeness. And the key point here, anyway, is that unless men themselves value fatherhood positively then such assertions of female choosiness risk being welcomed by them as an excuse to run away from responsibility. All the state can then do is to chase paternity payments. Without the magic and mystery of Divine Fatherhood there may be less to catch the male imagination.

By itself state intervention to promote fatherhood or renegotiation of parenthood seems unlikely to ever be very effective. It is too centralised, impersonal and distant from the detailed circumstances of people's lives. Religious culture by contrast operates locally, and within face-to-face groups. It encourages boys to be responsive, as they grow up, to the needs of family life going on daily around them, and then as men to the feelings of women who manage the families. This gives a directness and flexibility and sensitivity to relations between the sexes which can promote informed mutual understanding and tolerance. The machinery of state cannot do this. Indeed the opposite applies, in that possibilities for mutual misunderstanding are multiplied. Precisely because it is so centralised, state action is vulnerable to capture by determined interest groups intent on propagating their own ideologies. Recent social policy in the UK has been disproportionately influenced by idealistic dogmatists who insist that men and women are just the same, with identical reproductive strategies and natural investment in family life, so that it is only (patriarchal) culture which makes them behave differently. This approach hinders understanding.

Churches teach men to recognise their original nature and then work hard to reshape it. State-sponsored idealism simply urges them to deny it, and such denial of sexual nature seems to breed chaos and conflict. For unless differences are acknowledged, they cannot properly be dealt with. Little wonder that domestic negotiations become more fractious and fraught every year, and more people opt out of families altogether - including I suspect into homosexual identities, where difference *is* permitted. Homosexuality has become a refuge from the sex war. And while sexual confusion spreads and deepens, positive images of fatherhood fade.

Rekindling the spirit

If women were happy with these trends in family life then there would not be much to worry about. But the signs are that many, possibly most, are not. For them, having the support of a committed male partner is important. Many feminist commentators who in the past emphasised the paramount significance of female economic independence are now busily reconstructing fatherhood. This shift of priorities shows that time is now right to revive ailing religious conventions. Rediscovery is in the air. When Fay Weldon stands up to champion the Church of England then nothing is impossible.

A recreation of fatherhood is already underway in US churches, where evangelical movements such as 'Promise-Keepers' - which mobilises men to pledge fidelity to their partners - are making an impact on behaviour and public opinion. Fidelity is coming back into fashion. We should not expect identical developments in the UK. Religious observance here has contracted to a much lower level than reached in the US, and interest is more rooted in local community and less in large-scale campaigns. But it is worth noting that in spite of the mass-character and male face of Promise Keepers it appears to be wives and mothers and girlfriends who are the prime movers in getting men to go along to rallies. The sexual mechanics of religious conversion are traditional.

We may never witness this style of movement in the UK, but churches are beginning to understand what is happening to men. This is most true at grassroots in rundown localities where material deprivation combines with inappropriate state policies to render fatherhood extremely difficult. The *Mayflower Family Centre* in Canning Town is in the front line here. A veritable ship of hope and discovery in a sea of despair, it is patiently helping the local community to find out how religion can repair damage done to family life. Such ventures could take heart from the election of George Bush, who is expected to unlock state funding of social programmes operating through 'faith-based' organisations. If this sort of partnership works in the US, then its adoption in UK seems much more likely - whatever party is in power. Promotion of fatherhood is surely a prime candidate for such funding. But first we need some research on its spiritual dimension. The quicker that this gets underway here, the sooner we could institute appropriate action.

Ch.7
THE IMPORTANCE OF GRANDMOTHERS[1]

[This book] brings together a collection of personal reflections on what it means to be a grandmother in contemporary society, and views on how the role may be evolving.

We can safely assume from the outset that it will have changed a good deal in living memory, because family life in general has gone through radical transformations. Two sets of factors have been particularly important here. Firstly, developments in medical technology have helped to increase control over reproduction, so having a family can more easily be timed and scaled to fit in with other activities. Secondly, the growth of citizenship, as manifest in the multiplication of state supports, has meant that being a parent no longer need entail such dependence as before on relatives, friends and neighbours. Basic social security has become separated from community ties and obligations. Over the last third of a century these two major influences have combined to give people a larger choice of lifestyles, and thereby to encourage experimentation with new forms of household and family relationship.

Most commentaries on the ensuing lifestyle revolution have not touched on grandparents. But over the last few years there has been a surge of interest in grandparenting - prompted mainly by concern over the possible effects on children of new styles of

---

[1] This chapter is a shortened version of the preface to the collection which appeared first as *Grandmothers of the Revolution*, published in London by Hera in 2000, and is currently available as *Grandmothers: Changing the Culture*, (2002) New Brunswick: Transaction.

parenting - and in the part that grandparents might play or be playing as saviours of family life.

In response to these concerns, the Institute of Community Studies and National Centre for Social Research carried out a survey to get some idea of the current role played by grandparents in British society. This has given us a solid general picture of how the role is now acted out, plus some fascinating hints about how it may be changing.[2] However one survey, conducted over one short period, cannot really tell us much about trends. To get more insight into questions of how the role is adapting to new family behaviour it seemed essential to ask people who have been grandparents through the lifestyle revolution to make some personal assessments.

The accounts which follow here will help to give our research the historical dimension it lacks. This will go beyond clarifying the part played by grandparents. It also involves providing commentaries on the wider transformation of family and sexual behaviour. No realistic assessment of a radical change in lifestyles can be started until it has been tested in all stages of life. Young people are usually more willing to adopt novel ideas, especially those which challenge authority structures and give short-cuts to independence. But until new ideas have been adapted to the needs of other age-groups too, and can be seen to allow co-operation between generations, they cannot be regarded as viable. Only as the cohort leading the revolution itself moves through the life-cycle does it become possible to see which of its practices are ephemeral and age-specific, and which are more general and sustainable.[3]

We are arriving at this defining stage now for the libertarian revolution which was launched in the sixties. The postwar babyboom cohort has started to become grandparents and take

---

[2] Main report of which is Dench and Ogg, 2002.
[3] I have argued this at greater length in chapter 5 above.

on senior family positions. So we can now begin to see how far they will continue innovating and casting aside tradition, and how far the logic of their new roles may lead them back towards rediscovery and reassertion of traditional ways. It is an important moment of truth.

But why grand*mothers?*

The Rousing of Mother Nature

This opportunity for appraisal of social revolution coincides very handily with the rise of exciting new intellectual models, offering additional dimensions of analysis. The new discipline of Evolutionary Psychology, springing from the work of the late William Hamilton, has seriously challenged the traditional dichotomy between 'culture' (society) and 'nature'. This inevitably changes the way that we look at the sixties revolution. That was based on assertion of the power of human thought to transcend material factors, and to freely invent new futures. But as the wheel of revolution turns it is these new materialist theories which seem to offer the neater explanations of how society works. In particular, they are producing very stimulating insights into the part that women, and female nature, may have played in the formation of society.

One of the key debates here revolves, aptly enough, around the 'grandmother hypothesis'.[4] This debate springs out of scholarly efforts to understand the menopause. Human beings are one of the very few species where female fertility does not continue up to the end, or near the end, of the normal life-span. Elephants and whales share this. Excellent company!

The existence of the menopause is almost certainly linked with

---

[4] See in particular Sarah Hrdy, 1999.

the importance of long-term mothering in species where the young are dependent for a long period. Mothers who have children late in life cannot hope to rear them all, and may die even younger themselves in the attempt. However, menopause may also, perhaps even more revealingly, be related to grandmothering - and an overlapping of mothering in two generations. A mother with young children whose own mother is still alive, and not tied down by young children of her own, can expect crucial help during the early years when her infant offspring are most demanding.

As a result, those women genetically programmed to lose their fertility relatively early in their lives may prove more likely to have descendants who thrive and survive to have offspring of their own - who then pass on those genes. Thus the evolution of the menopause may be part of the evolution of human family behaviour.

There is more. Most evolutionary psychologists are reluctant to speculate too far on this, but it does seem extremely likely that the key role occupied by grandmothers within family groups will have given them immense influence on the development and operation of community life more generally. We know from historians and anthropologists that grandmothers are extremely important as repositories and transmitters of culture. As noted by Marc Bloch:

> Before the institution of the newspaper, the primary school, and military service, the education of the youngest living generation was generally undertaken by the oldest living generation. In rural village societies, because working conditions kept mothers and fathers away almost all day, especially during the summer period, the young children were brought up chiefly by their grandparents; so that it is from the oldest member of the household that the memory of the group was mediated to them. ... Until the introduction

of the first machines, it was grandmother who was the mistress of the household, who prepared the meals, and who, alone, was occupied with the children. It was her task to teach the language of the group. (1953: p.41)

Grandma knows best

If transmitter, then why not formulator too? No other category of family member could have been even half as well-placed, or disposed, to reflect on and assess the fundamental social values and rules which make community life possible. Consider the following. Grandmothers are generally the oldest members of a family group, with the greatest accumulation of personal experience. As women, their reproductive strategy entails long-term concern for the well-being of those around them. So they will also store knowledge about, and care about, the lives of many others in all age and sex categories.

On top of this, because they are (usually) no longer fertile themselves (and often widowed anyway) they are, more than old men, ideally suited to stand above or outside of the reproductive marketplace and to take an inclusive and integrating view of personal relationships. Looked at in this light, they are far better qualified and motivated than anyone else to devise reasonably objective schemes for the orderly management of family and sexual relations, which other family members could find acceptable.

Thus it is grannies who are typically the guardians of the common good and moral codes embodying this. They are the family peace-makers, match-makers and advisers. And while the primary reference of the principles they uphold will be inside families it is generally fairly obvious in most societies that wider moral systems, shaping relations between families and between other groups in the community, and informing law and religion, are themselves rooted in the rules of family life and its moral economy. All in all, the grandmother hypothesis provides ample encouragement for the general idea (which I have myself explored in an earlier book – Dench 1996a) that it is women, and especially older women, who are the main authors of human culture and architects of social structure.

Do not be misled by the fact that cultures generally represent men as central. Much of this public 'theatre of patriarchy' may be myth, covering and compensating for men's actual marginality and helping to steer them into useful activity and commitment.

Some such refurbished notion of mother nature, or perhaps grandmother nature, as a fundamental aspect of society (rather than as something opposed to it) seems to be in the ascendant at the moment. It certainly appears capable of attracting wide acceptance. Not only does it build on the solid achievements of down-to-earth feminism over the last few decades in identifying contributions made by women to social development. It also helps to exorcise another, thoroughly obscurantist tradition of feminism influential over the same period, namely the Flat-Earth tendency which resolutely denies human sexual differences and attributes all variations in behaviour to 'social construction'.

This latter tradition, itself a legacy of sixties idealism, has arguably done much to delay the emergence of popular new conventions for family organisation, compatible with modern realities. The revolutionary battle cry that 'family' is just an instrument of male bourgeois cultural oppression still echoes in the corridors of Whitehall and Westminster, where it continues to trigger panic among policy-makers. If anything can silence this ghost, and usher in much-needed rehabilitation of consensual family policy, it is Grandmother Nature.

The collection

This volume taps into a selection of grandmothers' experience of contemporary family life, and gives an indication of their concerns. This is not the place for me to analyse contributors' views along either of these axes. Both as a man and non-grandparent I have to be careful not to influence too closely how particular chapters are read. They must speak for themselves. But I cannot refrain from making the general observation that much of what is expressed in many of them - in particular belief in the paramount importance of families in society, not just for the sake of their members but also for the common good - seems to run counter to received opinion about 'what women want' in modern society. The contents of this book clearly suggest to me an effective exclusion of older women's voices and views from influential contemporary social policy debates.

Recovering a voice

Older women belong at the heart of cultural and social debate. But in the west we have allowed their voices to become muffled and ignored and this represents, notwithstanding the lavish and visible attention given to the interests of younger women, a net diminution in women's position. In more traditional societies the public participation of women may often be minimal. But most women in them are accorded high status and respect, especially on moral questions. Many also exercise considerable influence through sons and husbands, and as family managers, on the conduct of wider public affairs.[5] The fading of this influence in the west, together with dismantling of the wider family systems through which it operates, constitute a lingering legacy of the sixties.

---

[5] This was the situation as recently as mid-nineteenth century in the 'old' Bethnal Green explored by Michael Young and Peter Willmott. (1957) Matriarchal grandmothers (known as Mum to their offspring) were at the centre of community life, where they exercised considerable influence over practical matters of family members' employment and housing, as well as personal relations. They occupied a pedestal of respect which no politician (and no man) could hope to emulate.

Such exclusion may have a point in the early stages of social revolution, when generations are divided on many issues and opposition to change by elders may be based solely on dogma. But that no longer applies in this case. The great majority of older women in the west, certainly the grandmothers, now have close personal experience of 'new family' life. Their views are grounded, and in no way out of touch. It is the current wave of grandmothers who, against a background of declining public respect for the 'private realm' of family life, have done much to hold families together during the last twenty to thirty years. They are not easily shocked; and if anyone knows what is possible in modern situations, and what the basic rules for sustainable family life need to be, then they are the experts. They are in the vanguard in making this revolution work.

Research in countries which are ahead of us in exploring these issues suggests that the cultural gap which undoubtedly existed between generations in the seventies and eighties is now narrowing fast, as shown for example the work in France of Claudine Attias-Donfut, who is herself a contributor to this volume. The young are less radical; the old less reactionary. So there may be much less basis now for generation conflict, and no need for dogmas.

Where dogma can I suspect still be found though is among those hard-line political modernisers who have exploited differences in family values as a pretext for strengthening the role of the state in relation to ordinary families. It is their centralising reflex - which prefers to do things in the name of families, than to allow families the resources and rights to make their own choices within broadly agreed conventions - that is now beginning to look out of touch with the realities.

We should not be surprised at this. There have been several periods in the past when radical change in family life has been promoted, and manipulated, by political elites. But it is families, with older women in the vanguard, who end up defining the terms of eventual reconciliation between public and private lives. And it is with families as the leading partner, and state as their servant.[6]

Shortly after the last election I made the following observations:-

> This [neglect of the 'private realm' of family life] is arguably the single most important factor behind current alienation of ordinary people from politicians, ... Ironic as it may seem in the light of Labour Party performance and its closeness to the modernising movement, many older women appear to have voted Labour in 1997 in despair at the continuing failure of the Conservatives to come up with measures to match their pro-family rhetoric. ...
> Older women are a large and growing sector of the electorate. In 1992 they kept the Conservatives in power against the pollsters' predictions. Most are probably by nature more in tune with Tory worldviews, and this more than anything probably accounts for Labour's long exile in the wilderness. If Labour is to have any hope at all of keeping their vote at the next election it will need to re-examine its attitude in government towards the private realm. (1997: p.54)

These remarks are becoming ever more pertinent, as New Labour starts to run out of goodwill. The choice moreover is fairly simple. A government which neglects to listen to grandmothers, and regards them as stuck in the past, does not itself deserve and cannot expect to have much of a future.

---

[6] See for example Mount, 1982

Ch.8
GRANDPARENTS ARE BACK[1]

Grandparents are back. For around a generation, from the early 1970s to the latter 1990s, older people in Britain only really figured publicly as pensioners and patients in hospital queues: as citizens needing and generally deserving care and support. It was of course understood that many of them were grandparents, and had a family life. Just indeed as most families had people in them who were grandparents. But this was not regarded as having any significance outside of the family. It was certainly not something that policy-makers, journalists or more than a tiny fraction of social scientists bothered to think about. Amazing as it now already seems, throughout a period when all serious conversations about life were peppered with admonitions to connect the private and public realms, the personal and the political, families were largely kept out of sight and grandparents certainly had no place. No one even noticed that they were missing. As Claudine Attias-Donfut and Martine Segalen put it (1998), grandparents were the *grandes oubliés* of modern society.

Then a little while ago the lid on the oubliette was lifted. Grandparents found themselves allowed onto the policy stage, and quickly moved up everyone's agenda. Now we see grandparents as supplementary teachers, binding schools into local communities, or as colonising and socialising influences on sink estates. Grandparents portrayed as Stakhanovites of childcare, and saviours of broken families. Grannies as mentors for (unrelated) single mothers. Broadsheet editors coming out as grandparents.

---

[1] This chapter was originally produced in 2001 as a working paper, 'The changing face of British grandparenting', for *Grandparents Plus*. Bibliographic references have been updated for this present collection.

Government ministers resigning to spend more time as one. Grandparenating pages multiplying in magazines and on the airwaves. Grandparent chic wherever we look. A whirlwind of public interest has lifted grandparents and rehabilitated them almost overnight.

But because it has been so sudden, we still do not know all that much about what modern grandparenting means, nor indeed why it has become so salient again. We do not even know whether what grandparents *do* has changed very much. There is talk of change, and of the new importance of the role. But when something has been neglected for a while, and then rediscovered, it is very hard until the excitement dies down to distinguish between changes in the thing itself and changing attitudes or perceptions towards it.

We have carried out several pieces of research at the *Institute of Community Studies* (ICS) to help find out what is actually going on. In 1998 we collaborated with the *National Centre for Social Research* (NCSR) to include some questions on grandparents in their annual *British Social Attitudes* (BSA) survey. Findings were presented as a chapter in the 16th BSA report (Dench et al., 1999) and then in a fuller ICS report (Dench & Ogg, 2002) and in a variety of shorter reports. There had been no earlier studies in Britain with which we could compare our findings; therefore we could not draw firm conclusions from that survey about change over time. To help rectify this we also collected together a book of personal reflections by a selection of grandmothers on the role in different generations in their families (Dench, 2000). Lately we have also carried out a more intensive investigation with NCSR among some of the respondents in the 1998 survey. A first report on these findings has just been produced (Snape, Arthur & Dench, 2002).

When put alongside the recent work done elsewhere, this does begin to give us some picture of contemporary British grandparents. But on the crucial matters of change in grandparenting practice there are many things which remain unclear. It is rather easier to see why people have become interested in the issues, and what their concerns may tell us about changes in society and family life generally, than to come up with authoritative answers to specific questions about what grandparents *do*.

Even on apparently straightforward questions such as why public interest has been aroused, though, we have to acknowledge that things may not be quite as they seem. For example, there are several public concerns which manifestly seem to be driving interest in the role of grandparents. At the top of the list, and impinging closely on public policy, there are the questions of how much childcare is done by grandparents and how, in order to bring mothers back as quickly as possible into the labour market, this contribution might be increased. Not far behind these, and taking in a whole cluster of social policy and family law issues, there is interest in the role grandparents can play in protecting children during and after the trauma of family breakdown.

On such matters as these the rationale for current public interest in grandparenting is fairly obvious. But what is not so self-evident, and is often not addressed, is precisely why such concerns should have emerged when they did. Working mothers have needed heavy childcare support for decades. Family breakdowns have been increasing, and exciting public anxiety, for almost as long. So why start now looking to grandparents for solutions? A common response here would be to suggest that towards the end of the last century there was a loss of confidence in the durability of recent social change. Specifically, there was anxiety over whether the welfare state could go on providing personal supports via citizenship. So people were thinking again about family-based provisions. Faith in modernisation and new lifestyles slipped a little.

But these answers are not enough. All they really do is to restate the shift, without explaining it. Why should belief in the state, or progress, have started to fade when it did, when it could have done that at any time in the previous twenty or so years? It is more than just a *fin-de-siècle* effect. All of these suggested reasons have pertinence, and draw attention to an aspect of what is happening. Somehow though they fail to dispose of the main question. More is needed.

To locate the missing ingredients I think that we need to widen the net and look at a broader set of factors than are usually considered. It is the point at which to follow ourselves the precept about connecting the personal and the political. For the most adequate explanation for the timing of rediscovery of grandparents surely lies in the realm of collective life-cycle. There have been many important changes in family life since the early nineteen-seventies, and these have provoked qualms and resistance from the outset. What makes the late nineties so important in this respect, and the invoking of grandparents so telling, is that this is when the generation which has led the lifestyle revolution all the way through, recasting convention in new forms, itself started to enter grandparenthood in appreciable numbers. The cohort which had become used to having the world defined through its own eyes, now started to see things as grandparents. The 'end of the century' is also a generation after the turbulent 1970s.

Thus increasingly we have in senior family positions people with direct involvement in pioneering 'new' family behaviour, and so with a public legitimacy to assess and reconsider the underlying values. It may be this transition, rather than factors operating outside of the ranks of grandparents themselves, which is bringing these matters into public debate. We may be moving into a process by which the post-sixties revolution works its way into the last main stage of its advocates' life-cycle. This will by definition entail some adjustment of existing grandparental rules to new values. But the experience of being a grandparent is bound also to have an influence in turn on those values themselves. So what we are witnessing probably represents much more than the impingement on grandparents of a few issues relating to parenting deficits or childhood pathologies. It is, I suspect, the final act in an extended drama of cultural innovation, which is now approaching its climax. Grandparents are not merely caught up in social change. They are still driving it.

And they hold the map. The new family lifestyles that have developed since the early seventies now need pulling together into a coherent system capable of linking the interests of all generations. If this cannot be done, these lifestyles are not viable in the long term. And it is grandparents, who have lived through other life stages, who are best placed to make key judgements about what aspects of family life are crucial, and what changes are sustainable. This I think is the underlying meaning of the current public fascination with grandparenting. When taken into account it can illuminate much that would otherwise remain ambiguous or obscure, and perhaps help us to avoid misinterpreting some processes altogether.

Help for working mothers

One area where there may be a particular danger of missing what is going on is that of childcare. Our BSA98 survey data showed that remarkably high proportions of respondents, across all age and sex categories, believed that a major role for modern grandparents lay in looking after grandchildren in order to help mothers get back to work quickly. This is a line that has been peddled vigorously by politicians in recent years, so it would seem reasonable to conclude that popular attitudes are being shaped here by public pressures, and are moreover leading to changes in behaviour. It is frequently stated in the burgeoning articles and programmes dealing with grandparents that the modern world is requiring them to become ever more heavily involved with their grandchildren, and that their burden is far greater than that carried by previous generations. A newspaper poll carried out last year led to the conclusion that many grandparents regarded themselves as the new helots, unable to escape the imperious rule of their offspring, and lacking even the right to complain.

But much of this does seem questionable. In our own study we did not ask respondents how much help they *wanted* to give their children, only how much they did actually provide. On the basis of those findings we would be inclined to say that the amount of childcare currently done by British GPs, after adjustments are made for different phrasing of questions, is unlikely to be higher than that done in other European countries, and very possibly is rather less. There are also strong indications that the total load of childcare is less evenly distributed than elsewhere, with a few GPs doing a lot while many do hardly anything at all. This contrast may itself be one factor encouraging those who are active to feel that they are heavily burdened. Overall, and drawing on the findings of other surveys too, it does seem as though GPs in Britain may well feel that they are doing more than they really are.

In the first analysis of our data, published in the BSA report, we did not bother much about this comparative dimension, and concentrated on trying to sort out the factors currently determining the amount of grandparental input in Britain. Work commitments were obviously important, so we analysed the frequency of childcare support given against the work status of grandparent respondents themselves, plus of the mothers of grandchildren. We assumed we would find that the pattern of grandparental support would be related both to mothers' needs - the 'demand' - and to grandparents' availability to help out - the supply. But what the figures seemed to show was that although there is a definite link between the amount of childcare done by grandparents and mothers' working status, there is no clear pattern in relation to *grandparents'* work. The demand-side appeared dominant.

Even here the pattern was not straightforward. Least childcare by grandparents overall was done where mothers were not working – where need for help was therefore less. However, the most was done where mothers were working only part-time. This finding probably indicated that mothers working full-time are the most likely to be able to use nursery places and childminders, rather than relying just on family ties. But those grandparents who were involved in looking after the children of full-time working mothers also appeared to find it a rather less satisfactory experience. This suggested that grandparents are most likely to get involved (and to say yes if asked) where the load is not too great and can be fitted in smoothly with the other parts of their lives. So supply-side factors are relevant too, in that family negotiations around childcare may help to steer mothers into part-time working. The flexible nature of part-time work meshes better with family life, and a whole tranche of measures – from grandparents being most thoroughly involved, and feeling closest to children and grandchildren, to being happiest in their role – were clearly linked with it. Where mothers are working part-time, grandparents clearly feel needed and useful, and have regular contact with grandchildren – including some time alone with them – but without becoming overwhelmed by it all.

Subsequent analysis of the data has confirmed our general conclusion about this compatibility of part-time work with family care of grandchildren. But it has also shown that the supply side considerations, and factors in grandparents' lives, may be more important than we appreciated and have implications we did not consider.

When coming to look at the findings in more detail we found a flaw in our earlier analysis, in that it had not allowed sufficiently for differences between grandfathers and grandmothers. If these are separated and treated separately they show entirely different patterns. Full-time working grandfathers have more contact with grandchildren than do non-working, and claim to do more childcare too. What this probably means in practice though is that working grandfathers are more likely to have partners who do not need to work, or at any rate full-time, and so would themselves be free to take on more childcare. Such grandfathers would therefore live in households where there is more coming and going of grandchildren, and would be able to claim frequent involvement themselves - even if this was only indirect and marginal. It would certainly be more than full-time working grannies could manage. For their part, full-time working grandmothers recorded less childcare than others. But once grandmothers and grandfathers are pooled together these differences are cancelled out, and the significance of grandmothers' work status is obscured.

So we then carried out further computations looking at the combined work status of mothers and grandmothers (of working age) only. The results proved extremely revealing. To start with, there were actually fewer cases where the mother worked but not the grandmother, than the other way round in which only the grandmother worked. This gave an early sign that the working status of grandmothers was at least as important a consideration as that of mothers. Following this we identified four main patterns in relations between work status and grandparental involvement with grandchildren, which changed our view of what is going on. The main pattern of these findings is laid out in table 1, on the following page. Numbers in some categories are quite small – after removal of all the non-relevant cases like grandfathers, and grandmothers over 60. But the differences shown are strong enough to survive this.

At one end of the spectrum – in the left-hand column - where grandmothers are working but the mothers are not, we have a situation of low demand for childcare combining with low supply of grandparental time. Such grandmothers appear to be in a very strong position to play the role on their own terms and derive maximum pleasure from it. They saw their grandchildren very often, recorded by far the highest levels of satisfaction with the role, and general closeness to grandchildren, and in addition felt that they had a reasonable say in their upbringing. However, they did little formal childcare. They also gave more money than other grandmothers to their children and grandchildren.

The simple fact of working clearly has an empowering effect on grandmothers. For when we look at the cases in which neither grandmother nor mother is working – in the right-hand column - that is where there is low demand but high supply, then there are evident signs of increased childcare done, along with reduction in satisfaction, presumably because it is harder to say 'no'. A little more childcare is done, but casual contacts are fewer, and agreement with grandchildrens' upbringing, closeness to grandchildren plus general satisfaction with the role are all markedly lower.

Table 1.
Grandmothers' experiences according to combined work status
(column %)

Who works?	GM only	Mother FT	Mother PT	Neither M/GM
Agrees strongly that GP role very rewarding	86	52	70	73
Feels very close to GC	89	75	79	74
Sees GC several times a week	60	36	63	26
Looks after GC under 12 in day at least every week	15	27	48	25
Takes GC under 12 to/from school several times a month	(25)	(33)	(35)	(17)
Looks after GC under 12 in evening at least every week	15	22	28	17
Has say in how GC brought up	38	29	56	36
Has agreed most of the time with how GC brought up	38	13	51	23
(n - 100%) base figures	29	23	50	23

Then there are cases where both grandmother and mother are working. These have been sub-divided further according to whether the mother is full-time or part-time. Only the mother's detailed working status is used here because there are not enough cases to allow fuller division, and very few grandmothers work full-time if the mother is working at all. In those cases where grandmothers are working full-time, most mothers are not - which may itself say something about the importance of the supply side factors.

The split between full and part-time working mothers revealed some crucial differences. Where mothers are full-time we have a situation in which demand for grandparental childcare is potentially very high - though it can be less if the mother uses a nursery or childminder - while the supply is, at best, limited. The result is that grandmothers are more active in childcare than where mothers are not working at all. But only a little more. And against that they are much less in agreement with upbringing - perhaps related to the use of childminders and nurseries - have less say in it, do not feel very close to their grandchildren and above all have a far lower level of satisfaction with the grandparent role. So there are definite indications of stress in this group.

On the other hand, where mothers are working only part-time there appears to be a much greater involvement of grandmothers, even though they are working too. Levels of childcare are the highest, social contact is also frequent, say and agreement in upbringing are the highest, and closeness to grandchildren is reasonably high. Respondents' satisfaction with the grandparent role is only average, however, and below the levels for grandmothers where mothers are not working. So there are only relatively minor indications of stress here. Grandmothers where mothers are working part-time do seem to achieve a reasonable balance of involvement and satisfaction, while carrying out a large portion of the direct childcare which is actually done by grandparents.

A new generational division of labour?

What is perhaps most striking about these findings overall is that the role is enjoyed most where mothers are not working, and not making demands, and most of all where the grandmother is herself working and able to pick and choose what she does. This suggests quite powerfully that we may be wrong to assume that the public debate on grandparents' role has been triggered by rising demand, that is as a result of changing behaviour among mothers, and their desire to get back to work as soon as possible or by related shortages in state or commercial childcare provisions.

Given our findings, market imbalance in family childcare may be increasingly a matter of supply, and the outcome of changing behaviour of grandmothers. By pursuing their own careers more, and staying on longer in their jobs, they may be less available to help daughters and daughters-in-law as much as grannies did in the past. In reality demand may actually be falling - with many more women having fewer children, later in life, or none at all - but with supply falling even faster.

We cannot test this argument as we do not have equivalent data for the past. We know from ethnographic studies, and from anecdotal sources like our own recent collection of personal testimonies, that grandmothers in the past were often rather taken for granted by working mothers as sources of childcare (Neate, 2000). Many mothers much prefer to use a grandmother than to put children in a nursery, and would not go to work at all otherwise. But they have assumed that their mothers would help out. Indeed, many of the women who led the movement towards giving work greater salience in women's lives were only able to do so because their own mothers were free to help them.

It may be this which has changed most over the last few years. The main trend in women's employment since the seventies has been the expansion of 'careers' as opposed to mere jobs, and the correspondingly greater involvement in the labour market of middle-class women. This brings us back to life-cycle, and to the movement now of 'sixties girls' into senior family roles. Grandmothers of present-day young grandchildren are much more likely to have interesting jobs, which may well be better paid too than those which their daughters have or could get. On top of this, many of them have spent all of their adult lives at work, and have never been engaged in extensive childcare anyway. The traditional division of labour between generations involved older women in the family staying at home to look after children while their daughters went out to work. This may be facing an unprecedented challenge as female work becomes increasingly middle class. The public perception that grannies are in demand, plus their own claims to be under great pressure, may in fact reflect a growing tendency for grannies themselves, those in the middle class at any rate, to say 'no'.

In short, what may be new therefore is not the pressure on grannies, but their resistance to it. The revolutionary generation of women which has challenged and adapted convention as it passed through earlier life-stages is now in revolt against the traditional expectation of daughters - which they exercised themselves as daughters - for family childcare support. And this would help to explain our findings that, at a time when grandparents claim to be providing a lot more help than previous generations, many do not seem to be doing very much at all. There may be many families in which wholly new types of negotiations and battles are emerging. It is ripples from these private revolutions which may be what is prompting the public debate.

If this is so, it would require different approaches to issues of childcare. Calling for grandmothers to step in more may simply be putting the clock back to an era of Babushkas. Britain is a country in which women's labour market participation has matured to a point where grandmothers now have useful and attractive work options that prevent them from being automatically available for childcare. New conventions are needed, such as that being worked out by Janet Nelson, whereby mothers and grandmothers, along with fathers and other relatives too, share childcare in a way that allows all of them to follow a career and outside interests too (Nelson, 2000). We do not yet have a culture in which women, like men, can expect to have a life outside of the home which is similar to their parent's. In the past those women who have had successful careers have tended either to be childless or to get support from other women in their families, mothers and even daughters too, who almost by definition did not enjoy equivalent opportunities or encouragement themselves. If many more women are to have careers, greater emphasis will have to be put on ways in which different generations can share both work and caring activities.

This may already be underway. Our BSA98 findings reveal an optimal balance - involving high rates of childcare by grandparents, combined with higher-than average levels of role satisfaction - where both grandmother and mother were working part-time. By contrast, the least happy grandmothers (and also less active as childcarers) were those where mothers were working full-time. If such grandmothers are not working themselves, they are then liable to become heavily tied down by childcare. If they are working themselves, they can still get drawn by their daughters' heavy needs into doing more than they would like. Both types end up stressed.

Proposals aimed at mobilising more care by grandparents have yet to catch up with this. Those grandmothers who say no to regular childcare, and who give money rather than provide direct help themselves, seem to be the ones who are happiest. Where there is choice, many grandmothers may be doing less than their children might like them to do, and almost certainly less than policy-makers concerned to put the mothers onto the labour market have bargained for.

The effects of family breakdown

Much of the preceding discussion on work patterns is rather speculative. We do not really know how the supports given by grandparents ten, twenty and thirty years ago compare with those given today. There is no equivalent information. And because the changes in grandparenting suggested above are only just breaking, it is bound to be some time before enough evidence to assess the argument can be pooled together, and the picture becomes clear.

On some other aspects of grandparenting we are however on firmer ground. In particular it does seem safe to say that the pattern of grandparenting is being influenced quite clearly by the growing instability of parenting relationships. The structure of supports given to parents and of contact with grandchildren is manifestly different where parents are not together. We do know, in great detail and very reliably, how conjugal and parenting ties have been changing over the last generation. It is therefore reasonable to assume that related aspects of grandparenting behaviour are shifting with them.

This shift has two main facets. Firstly there is an intensification of grandparental involvement. When parents are living together there are two adults in the household to share looking after the children. We know from domestic surveys in Britain that it is fathers who, even if not equally involved in childcare, provide the major overall support for mothers. To be precise here we should say mother's partner rather than father, as available evidence indicates that step-fathers are not much less active here. However, the key point is the negative one, that in single-parent households where (overwhelmingly) mothers do *not* have live-in help on hand, much greater demands are made on grandparents.

It may well be such cases that get reported as evidence for the supposed increase in grandparenting activities in Britain. Within the context of single-parenting or marriage breakdown, claims of over-burdened grandparents may well be true. It certainly has a psychological truth, because the greater and more urgent needs of a single parent mean that it is much harder for grandparents to say no. They will often feel steamrollered by their offsprings' plight, so that other things they wanted to do, or even other sets of grandchildren they might have wanted to spend more time with, are liable to get displaced. The normal procedures of family negotiation and reciprocity have to be put on hold. But grandparents do respond. It is noteworthy that in our BSA98 findings *all* of the grandmothers who reported that they had given up work in order to look after grandchildren did so to help out a lone parent.

However, not all grandparents experience the same effects. Breakdown of parenting does not just lead to increased demands. Other grandparents, usually those related through an absent or 'non-resident' parent, are likely to become more distant from grandchildren, and quite often to be cut off altogether. So while there may be an intensification of the role in some families, in others there is diminution. This brings us to the second consequence of parenting splits. This is that lineage is becoming increasingly significant in determining grandparents' experience, with those in the male line mainly losing touch. In relation to the cases of never-married single mothers, who represent a still-growing trend in Britain, there is also a growing category of grandparents through the father who do not even know of the existence of those grandchildren. For them the role does not exist.

Thus the steady growth of single-parenting and marriage breakdown in Britain is producing a noticeable polarisation in grandparenting behaviour. At one extreme there is a group of grandparents, overwhelmingly in the mother's line, who become heavily caught up in supporting activities, often at the expense of other elements in their lives. At the other extreme there are those, virtually always on the fathers' side, who are effectively excluded from playing much of a part, and sometimes have no contact with these offspring or knowledge of them. This represents a significant divergence, and almost certainly a considerable change. We know from ethnographic and cultural studies that there has long been recognition of stronger emotional attachment along maternal lines in Britain, as elsewhere. But we also know that paternal grandparents played a large part in people's lives too. The sharp divergence now resulting from family breakdown presents an obvious challenge to the bilineal tradition. It greatly reinforces underlyling matrilineal preferences, and weakens patrilineal ties even further.

Table 2 on the following page takes a few measures of grandparenting behaviour and attitudes from the BSA98 survey, and shows the effect on them of unstable parenting.[2]

---

[2] Only the responses of *grandparents* in the sample are dealt with here. For information on responses by grandchildren and parents see Dench et al., 1999, plus Dench & Ogg, 2002.

Table 2.
Grandparents' behaviour according to lineage and split
(Column %)

	Link through daughter		Link through son	
	1 Parents apart	2 Parents together	3 Parents together	4 Parents apart
Sees GC several times a week or more	44	32	30	18
Lives within 15 minutes of GC	40	32	37	26
Visits friends and relatives with GC (without parents) monthly +	30	13	13	5
Feels very close to GC	79	73	66	35
Looks after GC in day at least every month	68	61	48	37
Takes GC to/from school at least monthly+	34	22	15	3
Has/ has had say in how GC brought up	66	34	23	0
(n - 100%) base figures range	68-92	201-293	174-240	35-56

The middle columns (2 & 3) in Table 2 contain responses according to line of descent where parents are still together. The matrilineal line in this pair consistently indicates greater closeness, on all measures, though not very powerfully. The left-hand column (1) contains equivalent matrilineal responses, and the right-hand (4) patrilineal, for cases where parents of grandchildren are not together.

Arranging the columns in this way makes it very clear that there is a noticeable intensification of difference on virtually all measures, though in reality the differences will be even greater than this. [3]

The evidence for polarisation here is very strong. It is also consistent with the findings of a great mass of research focusing on the breakdown of marriage and its implications for other family relationships. The question which then arises, though, is whether and how far this manifest trend is sustainable. Are we moving into a new type of family structure. Or are we simply passing through a short-term perturbation?

It is more likely long-term. The modern welfare state, evolving alongside greater control over reproduction, has made it much easier for women to raise children if they wish without the participation of men. Single-parenting, meaning single-mothering, then develops over time into matrilineal descent-groupings with limited affinal ties to other families, and often needing to call on the state for material supports which its own members may be unable to provide. These supports are sometimes seen as replacement of fathers. For, contrary perhaps to the expectations of some 1960s visionaries, and perhaps above all because of the legalisation of abortion – as a result of which there are fewer unwanted children - there is decreasing call for the state to take over the maternal, caring side of family life. So a future family system of strong, emotionally self-sufficient (and perhaps even rather exclusive) matrilineal groupings, in which sexual partnerships remain weak, volatile and subject to continual choice, does not seem out of the question.

---

[3] A clue here is that the patrilineal 'not together' column contains fewer cases than the matrilineal equivalent. This is partly due to demographic factors, such as the later age at which men become parents. But it also reflects the fact that some patrilineal grandparents may not know of the grandchild or of their son's relationship. Also some may know of it but, because of the awkward circumstances, prefer not to declare it. If all such instances could be included in column 4 the overall rates of activity for this category would fall even lower than they have done.

But against that it has to be said that there are few signs that this is actually what most people want. It may be that some are holding back a little from a family lifestyle which is still not properly tested. The bandwagon may only just be creaking into motion. This is not impossible. However the more likely scenario is that after a period of experimental movement in that direction, there is already reluctance to travel much further. The growing interest in grandparents itself may partly reflect this, and be a first sign of reaction to this matrilineal and overtly matriarchal family culture. It may even be a pointer to where the reaction is coming *from*.

Taking the strain of change

The general point here perhaps is that there are no obvious beneficiaries of matrilineal shift. The polarisation it produces involves a narrowing of the support system which seems to leave all categories of family members feeling that they have lost something, and undermines their satisfaction in their roles.

To take matrilineal grandparents first, it is obvious that the salience of their role is increased where their daughter does not have a partner (plus kin through him) to help out. Their enhanced involvement can bring them closer to their grandchildren. But the additional activity does not seem to add up to greater satisfaction. It makes the role more like that of a parent, and the greater responsibility - at a time when they may have been expecting easier lives - can be a source of stress. Doing more often means doing too much.

This effect is shown in the following table. Where parents are not together, fewer matrilineal grandparents find the role rewarding, fewer find that they were in agreement with how their grandchildren were being brought up, and more wish that they could be freer of family obligations. (Caution is needed in interpreting the first two measures in the table, as they refer to respondents' overall evaluation of their role and some had grandchildren through more than one child. So we cannot be sure in those cases how much the broken parenting is influencing their views. However, if we just concentrate on those cases where there is only one grandchild, the pattern sharpens. But the numbers in columns become smaller and the significance of the differences plummets. So the full effect of breakdown may actually be muffled in this table.)

Table 3.
Grandparents' role satisfaction
(%)

	Link through daughter		Link through son	
	1	2	3	4
	Parents apart	Parents together		Parents apart
Agrees strongly that role very rewarding*	63	67	64	42
Would like to have life more free of family duties*	42	34	36	48
Has agreed most of the time with how GC brought up	34	42	34	12
(n) base figures range	68-92	201-293	174-240	35-56

- Measures here based on *general* measurements of role.

At the opposite extreme, patrilineal grandparents are liable to become cut off from grandchildren after parental breakdown. Given the stress experienced by overloaded matrilineal grandparents, this detachment might be seen as constituting a welcome break. This does not however seem to be the case. The evidence collected suggests that overall there is even greater role disappointment and dissatisfaction for them where parents of grandchildren are apart. Even fewer find the role rewarding, only a fraction feel in tune with their grandchildren's upbringing and even more expressed a desire for a freer life. What this adds up to on the paternal side appears to be considerable strain at under-involvement. Doing *less* means not feeling part of what is going on. So at both ends of the spectrum there is less enjoyment of the role.

Neither line of grandparents seems to have much to gain from further progress down the matrilineal road. But what about parents, and above all mothers? If the shift suited them, then it might still lead somewhere. Here the evidence is less direct, and less clear. Our survey did cover parents' views on grandparenting, but did not ask direct questions about their own satisfaction with arrangements. We have explored this in the smaller-scale, more intensive follow-on study, and the findings from that are starting to help make more sense of the survey data. But more analysis, including perhaps a new wave of research more focused on parents, is likely to be needed before the picture that appears to be emerging can be treated with full confidence.

What is coming out is that many single-parent situations are in reality quite short-term. In particular, single mothering by young women who have never cohabited with the fathers of their children turns out often to represent a prelude to a more settled relationship. Maternal grandparents frequently do provide intensive supports for such mothers. But there are problems for all. For grandparents, very heavy involvement is an obstacle to becoming *proper* grandparents - that is, who remain at a suitable distance from parental responsibility. Similarly for their daughters, a heavy grandparenting role constitutes a postponement of their own growing up and achievement of adult autonomy. The mothers themselves lose out in terms of an important feature of British culture. The single mother who remains heavily dependent on her parents stays a child to them. This is not so true for a separated mother who gravitates back to her own parents after the break-up of a relationship. But even then there may be a sense in which the mother and children together become children again in relation to the grandparents, as these become active parents again.

These more intensive arrangements can become long-term, and if this happens problems of status that are created can be mitigated by careful attention to boundaries, and in particular by clear rules about who makes decisions relating to the grandchildren. But there seem to be problems and tensions inherent in the situation. And these motivate mothers to find a partner and set up a conventional household, in order to reduce undue dependence on grandparents and allow them to take fuller control themselves over their own and children's lives.

New stages in the life-cycle

Thus what the matrilineal shift may really represent is another aspect of the contemporary *elongation of childhood*. With longer life-spans, reliable means of postponing reproduction, and general proliferation of lifestyle opportunities and choices, people are taking longer to decide what to do with their lives and then settling down to doing it. For increasing numbers of young women this seems to involve having children *before* finding a partner, or changing partners more easily and frequently than in preceding generations, or even extending the later stages of childhood into the early stages of parenthood. Perhaps it also represents some movement back towards pre-Victorian practices, to a family culture in which having a child (or, at least, getting pregnant) was regarded as a useful reason for settling down, rather than a consequence of it. An additional difference these days, of course, is that marriage is far from being the only means of becoming independent of parents. It is comparatively straightforward for a single mother to increase her autonomy by limiting further reproduction, taking full-time employment, and tapping into community and workplace supports such as nurseries.

This is evident not just from our detailed family case-histories, but also from the earlier survey data. These show that where parents had been separated only recently there was considerably more grandparental support to mothers than where they had been apart for longer. Clearly this is partly a matter of the age of grandchildren, and their needs. The youngest, most dependent, are likely to be involved in the most recent splits. But it is also consistent with a gradual development or recovery of maternal independence. Where parents are formally divorced, indicating an advanced state of post-breakdown settlement, the levels of grandparental support for mothers are not much greater than where parents are still together.

The period when really intensive grandparental involvement is required may not last very long, and may be gone through in one way or another by quite a large proportion of contemporary mothers - to be followed soon in most cases by 'settling down' with the childrens' fathers or new partners, and in some cases by longer-term female independence. Significantly, a higher proportion of divorced single mothers (than of merely separated) had full-time jobs. This shows that the self-reliance produced by paid employment does bring independence from parents as well (as is more often emphasised) as from men.

What evidence there is on fathers is even patchier. Matrilineal shift cuts out many men altogether. Some may accept this without much heartache, or even welcome it. A number of men are active however in seeking access and a share in their children's upbringing. This is sometimes at the instigation of paternal grandmothers, and a recent *Families Need Fathers* guide refers to the influence that grandparental concerns may have. As one grandchild is reported saying, "If it weren't for my grandparents I wouldn't have known who my dad was."(Secker, 2001: p.60) But in most cases we must assume that fathers do want to play a supporting role, and experience too a loss of satisfaction when they are excluded from doing so.

On the basis of the reactions briefly sketched out here it does seem safe to suggest that we are probably not witnessing a fundamental transition to a new type of family structure. Multi-generational matrilineal families, in which relationships with fathers and male sexual partners were treated as irrelevant, do not actually appeal to many people. If they did, we would expect to have picked up many more positive orientations towards them than we have. All the signs are that people living within family networks operating in this way are able to cope very well, and have close personal relationships with each other as a result. But we have not found any cases in our qualitative studies where coping is not combined with expressions of regret at what is being missed in terms of contacts and ties in wider family groupings. Maternal grandparents, and in particular grandmothers, are able to react to their daughters' needs as single mothers, and do step in with more intensive help than is generally given. But they do not see themselves and should not be seen as a sort of vanguard showing others the way to a new social order. Many are concerned at the lack of paternal involvement. If anything, their social attitudes seem to be a little more *conservative* than those of grandparents whose children are in stable relationships, and a little more anxious about the way that society appears to be moving.

Notwithstanding matrilineal shifts, the more general trend is likely to be in the other direction, towards *less* intensive involvement of grandmothers - reflecting their own increasing commitment to work and interests outside of their families - and a spreading of support more widely back across bilateral kinship networks. Grandmothers like to have frequent contact with their offspring so that they can watch them grow and feel confident that they are alright. Twice a week is often put forward as an ideal frequency of contact. The early, most active stage in grandparenting is at the same time a late stage of parenting, in which children are helped to become confident parents themselves. So grandmothers themselves desire and seek regular contact.

But it is only in situations of great or urgent need that most would want to take on a heavy involvement. We know that in the US, many grandparents are having to accept high levels of responsibility for grandchildren who have been let down by their parents. Intensifying marital breakdowns, commonly linked to drugs and serious poverty, and aggravated by limited community services, mean that more than one in twenty children under 18 now live in households headed by grandparents (Bryson &

Casper, 1999). There is a price to pay for this in terms of stress. But if the needs arose, there would be the same response in Britain too. That is part of a grandmother's nature.

Grandmother Nature

The rapid changes in family lifestyles that have taken place over the last generation are by no means over. But enough has already unfolded to give us some indications about what may be more, or less, possible. The revolution constitutes a form of natural experiment, through which we can see a little more clearly which aspects of the way we live are cultural and ephemeral, what is in our nature and more enduring, and how these different components may interact, overlap and indeed develop together.

In this natural experiment it is the generation that is now entering into grandparenthood which is the moving factor. It is they who as teenagers in the sixties began self-consciously to reject tradition and the authority of elders, then in the seventies pioneered new domestic lifestyles of their own. As they become grandparents themselves they confront the consequences of their radicalism from the other side of the barricades. If they find that there are elements of resulting lifestyles that they do not feel comfortable with, they will not be shy in saying so, and in making further innovations. It is too soon to say how this will actually pan out. But on the basis of recent research two or three tentative suggestions can be made.

Firstly it seems likely that where new technology has given us new opportunities, these are judged pragmatically. For example, greater control over reproduction has massive implications. It means that sexual activity no longer need tie women to child-bearing, so that that they can plan and invest in careers far more readily. It also means that people can stay free from responsibilities to others, and remain grown-up children for longer, if that is what they want. The early indications from our research are that insofar as new lifestyles multiply choice, the generation of revolution is staying young and pushing the revolution further. As it moves into senior family positions it retains the libertarian values that are held by younger people.

Where young grandparents do seem to be more cautious, and to draw lines, is where such choices have serious implications for family relationships, in particular those which impinge on the wellbeing of children. Younger grandparents do not seem greatly different from older when it comes to matters like the value of parents staying together while children are growing up. The underlying issue here seems to be that of security. Children are seen to fare better, and have their interests protected better, where there is a wide range of adults securely linked to them and with powerful obligations towards them. In the past marriage was seen to ensure the existence of two sets of kin allied around a commitment to the welfare of children - and not least to seeing that the 'other' set of kin did their bit too. One of the major disabilities of the state of illegitimacy lay in there not being a second (paternal) set of kin with conventional obligations to provide support and care, both to help and to *moderate* the power of those possessing effective custody and control over a child. There is much less emphasis on marriage now, outside of a small and dwindling church population. But among grandparents, and even among matrilineal grandparents heavily involved in supporting a single-mother, there seems to be a widespread feeling that it is much better for grandchildren to have two sets of kin rather than one. Stable parenting relationships are widely regarded as providing a guide to or guarantee of this.

Some visionaries in the seventies foretold that the blossoming welfare state would provide all of the support and security that children could want, and on a much more equitable basis than offered by families. But few people now seem to believe this, certainly ordinary people actively engaged in parenting. The most reliable and conscientious care is seen as coming from within a family - which is why most mothers definitely prefer family childcare where possible. The state can help, by providing supplementary supports and public scrutiny. When it does so though, it is behaving much like an additional set of kin, augmenting the range of care surrounding a child rather than replacing family responsibility. And few voices are now heard advocating that. The best security for children still comes from extending parenting and grandparenting and related family care as widely as possible.

This is a principle that *Grandparent Plus* holds dear. And learning it is something that comes for most people out of the practical experience of being a parent and grandparent. It is a clear example of where new grandparents seem likely to have modified their earlier more libertarian viewpoints and have turned their backs on revolution and conventions deriving from it. Accordingly this is one area where grandparents may have some disagreements with their own children in the early years of grandparenting, before those children have accumulated their own experience.

A third conclusion, which can be called that because the evidence pointing to it is much firmer than for the other issues just mentioned, is that - and again in the face of seventies' declarations and prognoses - there do seem to be enduring differences between men and women; fathers and mothers; grandfathers and grandmothers. These differences seem to have been sharpened rather than blunted by conventional denial of them. They remain undiminished among the youngest grandparents, certainly in their behaviour if not so obviously in some of their public attitudes.

Thus is it overwhelmingly and even increasingly grandmothers who show greatest interest in grandchildren, spend most time with them, put themselves out to look after them and are prepared to shape their lives to fit around their needs. Above all, it is grandmothers who are reported by grandchildren, and by the parents of grandchildren, as doing these things. One of the most striking findings to come out of our research is that although a number of grandfathers do claim to be quite involved, these claims are not substantiated by other categories of respondents. It seems likely that many grandfathers may actually feel that they are doing a lot, simply because they live in a household where there is a grandmother who does do a lot (Dench & Ogg, 2001: chapter 12). They are basking in a halo effect.

This conclusion gets some unexpected and very telling confirmation from our findings on step grandparents (ibid, chapter 11). At first sight, as a single category, step-grandparents appear to be broadly interested and involved with grandchildren, but at a less intense level than natural grandparents. However, when they are divided according to sex some clear differences emerge. The step-grandfathers turn out to be very much like other grandfathers on most counts, and if anything cluster towards the enthusiastic end of the spectrum. Step-grandmothers on the other hand record much lower levels of interest and activity: not just a lot lower than other grandmothers, but than all categories of grand*fathers* too.

The obvious inference to be drawn from this is that for grandmothers a close bonding from infancy - rooted in many cases perhaps in awareness of biological connectedness - is altogether more important than it is for grandfathers. Maternal relationships depend for their success on a level of identification, and shared understandings, that take much time and effort to create and sustain. Paternal are different. To be a reasonably successful father it may not be essential to have a close personal bond with children. What is probably more important is a good relationship with their mother. The really crucial aspects of fathers' roles may be, even more perhaps these days when men in families are more marginal and dispensable than in the past when they were usually around, those to do with helping a mother and backing her up. The male essentially plays a supporting role.

The reason why step-grandfathers can register such high levels of enthusiasm for their role may therefore be that it is the relationship with their partner which determines their role. They are likely to be with new partners they have recently committed themselves to. Thus a father and step-father, grandfather and step-grandfather, may all be very alike each other in their behaviour and feelings towards children. Unlike mothers, fathers could not until very recently ever be absolutely sure that they *were* the childrens' father. So the line between being a step-father and father is a thin one anyway. A man who changes partners is likely to accept her offspring into his world, and loosen his ties with existing children and grandchildren, much more readily than a woman. In our data, divorced grandmothers see their grandchildren as much or even more than other grandmothers do (ibid. chap. 12). Divorced grandfathers on the other hand see their grandchildren a lot less. Some of them have moved on meanwhile to become step-grandfathers, where their behaviour may be much more attentive because it is fitting in with a rhythm set by his current partner.

Being a grandfather is not so important and distinctive - either for the grandchild or the grandfather himself - as being a grandmother. We all knew this anyway. But this confirmation of the special value of grandmothers, along with the rehabilitation of grandparents generally as part of the final stage of lifestyle revolution, all come at a time when new understandings of human nature and culture may be revealing just how important grandmothering is. As I have noted elsewhere, the new discipline of evolutionary psychology has produced some very stimulating insights into the part that women, and female nature, may have played in the formation of society. One of the key debates revolves, aptly enough, around the 'grandmother hypothesis', which arises out of attempts to explain the menopause. Human beings are one of the very few species - elephants and whales are others - where female fertility does not continue up to the end, or even *near* the end, of the normal life-span. This is most unlikely to be a coincidence.

The existence of the menopause is almost certainly linked with the importance of long-term mothering in species where the young are dependent for an extended period. Mothers who have children late in life cannot hope to rear them all, and may die even earlier themselves in the attempt. Menopause helps to prevent this, and may also - and even more revealingly - be related to grandmothering, which forms an overlapping of mothering in two generations. A mother with young children whose own mother is still alive, and not tied down by young children of her own, can expect crucial help during the early years when her infant offspring are most demanding. As a result, those women genetically programmed to lose their fertility relatively early in their lives may prove more likely to have descendants who thrive and survive to have offspring of their own - who then pass on those same genes. The evolution of the menopause may be part of the evolution of human family behaviour.

This has implications for society more generally. It means that grandmothers will have had great influence throughout history not just as repositories and transmitters of culture, but as formulators of the values and rules which make community life itself possible. Grandmothers are usually the oldest members of a family group, with the greatest accumulation of personal experience. As women, their reproductive strategy entails long-term concern for the well-being of those around them. So they will also store knowledge about, and care about, the lives of many others in all age and sex categories.

On top of this, the menopause removes them from the reproductive marketplace, to a position where they can take a more inclusive and therefore integrating view of personal relationships.

Altogether, then, they are far better qualified and motivated than anyone else to devise reasonably objective schemes for the orderly management of family relations, which other members can find morally acceptable, and which provide a model for the organisation of most other social institutions. Thus it is grannies who are typically the guardians of the common good and moral codes embodying it. Grannies care. They can be seen as having both the incentive and opportunity to be the main authors of basic human culture. Grandmother nature probably lies at the very heart of our society and culture.

Recovering family life

The particular content of grandmothers' roles, and especially their material contribution to family welfare, varies a lot according to circumstances. In the most elementary of societies, where people live by hunting and gathering, grandmothers seem to be champion gatherers. They know best how to identify and find edible plants that provide families' staple diet. They have the time to go searching for them, and often collect a sizeable proportion of the food consumed. Families with grannies eat better. In most types of agricultural and industrial economy a grandmother is more likely to stay at home as a teacher/childminder so that mothers can spend time in the fields or factories.

In late industrialism, where skills take longer to acquire, we may be moving towards a new pattern, at least among better-off classes. Women have many fewer children, and these soon become caught up in social activities outside the domestic realm - where other family members are also spending more of their time. In such circumstances the material contribution that many grandmothers may make most usefully to their offspring's wellbeing and life chances may consist less of intensive, home-based childcare, and more of continuing pursuit of a remunerative career allowing transfer of additional financial resources to assist with grandchildren's maintenance and education. If mothers want family-based childcare, there will be a number of adults they can share bits of it with. As society itself evolves, so do the ways in which grandmothers can provide an umbrella of care.

In the moral realm though there may be greater continuity. This area is harder to explore, but it does seem that the value of grandmothers as sources of socialisation and moral instruction is hardly acknowledged now - except perhaps in the narrow context of rescuing children following breakdown of parental relationships.[4] Lifestyle radicalism banished the image of grandparents as founts of wisdom. But we may be neglecting this traditional role at our peril. It may be significant that it was during the period when grandparents were most 'forgotten' that a sense of social dislocation and anomie became so over-powering in British society. The place of family elders as trusted and respected advisors may be crucial to the sense that family life can impart to members of having a place in a sympathetic community, in a meaningful universe.

In this respect it will be fascinating to see whether grandparents regain a legitimate voice as they are rediscovered, and how they use it. Older women, grandmothers especially, belong at the centre of cultural and social debate, monitoring events to interpret and update the common good. For much of the last twenty years or more they have been displaced from this trustee role by a rebellious younger generation which did not heed them, in collusion with an interventionist state. But now *that* generation are becoming grandmothers themselves. As they do so, they seem to be asserting, from the other side now, that families do need grandparents after all.

There is every reason to anticipate that restoration of grandparents will include recognition of an advisory role for them, and a revival of inter-generational solidarity within families. Research in France, asking questions not yet directly addressed in Britain, indicates that young grandmothers are now much more in tune with their adult children on moral and social issues than with their own parents (Attias-Donfut & Segalen, 1998). The libertarian revolution fractured consensus, within families, along generation lines. But this fracture is now passing into history as the postwar parental generation dies off, taking no-longer-relevant values with it.

---

4 And even there it is sometimes *denied*, by social workers arguing that where parental breakdowns have occurred it is likely to be the grandparents' fault.

We cannot draw direct conclusions for Britain from this. But in our own research findings there are some indirect hints too that family moral coherence may be on the mend. Grandparents do not have formal authority. And in general terms, most people do not feel that grandparents as a category have much to teach younger family members. But inside actual families things look different. People do not regard the grandparents in their own families as out of touch. And for their part, most grandparents of young children see themselves and are seen by the parents as substantially in agreement over issues of upbringing. This is not so true of older grandparents. So there is some evidence of family reintegration taking place here too.

This is new. As recently as 1996, *Reader's Digest* published a guide to grandparenting which clearly assumed that a generation gap prevailed. The volume read as a manual designed to help out-of-touch grandparents to understand those strange younger generations: a sort of tourist guide preparing them for a journey to a remote, alien and altogether threatening country. Already this seems impossibly dated. The great majority of grandmothers now have personal experience of new family life, and indeed are the real experts in it. They are not easily shocked. They are the ones doing much to hold families together in an age which still has little public respect for them, who know what is and is not possible in modern situations, and who are in the vanguard of reconciling the individualist revolution with enduring realities of family life.

It is not grandparents any more who really need bringing up to date, but the agencies dealing with families and looking after their members' interests in an official world which has drifted off-track in an anti-family, universalistic reverie. A major legacy of social revolution is that the state can no longer even see real families. Families were defined in the 1970s as hostile to personal freedom and expanding citizenship rights. So official statistics since have focused mainly on households, that is clusters of citizens who by virtue of co-residence impinge on each others' personal claims on the state. Within this framework, families are conceptualised in terms of adults with co-resident minors dependent on them until they too become full citizens too. To the official mind, families are little more than citizen-farms.

The re-appearance of grandparents, regardless of what has prompted it, shows up the narrow limitations of this approach. Once grandparents come back into the frame, the importance in people's lives of family ties cutting across households has to be admitted. Then the way is wide open for recognition of extended family networks more generally.

The lineal relationship between grandparents and grandchildren does not exist in a vacuum - much as some commentators and policy-makers might like it to. It is part of a general lineage principle which informs a whole system of inter-personal bonding and support. This system has carried on, while in ideological exile, looking after most people's basic needs and providing their personal security. But its role has been played down and ignored by recent cohorts of legislators and administrators who have been suspicious of it, even fearful of it, and who thought that it might just go away. But it has not, and we need to be very grateful for this. For although the state can supplement the intimate and intricate web of care which kinship networks provide it cannot replace it, and it should not try. This I believe is the general lesson that is coming out of our research at the Institute on changing grandparenting practices, and which *Grandparent Plus* is now poised to put into action.

REFERENCES

Altman Y (ed) *Careers in the New Millennium*, Leuven/Amersfoort: Acco.

Attias-Donfut C & Segalen M (1998) *Grands-Parents: La famille a travers les generations*, Paris: Odile Jacob.

Batten M (1992) *Sexual Strategies*, New York: Tarcher/Putnam.

Billington R (1994) *The Great Umbilical: mothers, daughters, mothers*, London: Hutchinson.

Bloch M (1953) *The Historian's Craft*, New York: Vintage.

Bryson K R & Casper L M (1999) *Co-resident grandparents and grandchildren*, Washington: US Census Bureau.

Bunting M (1993) 'The lost generation', *The Guardian*, 7th September.

Burgess A (1997) *Fatherhood reclaimed*, London: Vermilion.

Burgess A & Ruxton S (1996) *Men and their children*, London: Institute for Public Policy Research.

Daly M (1979) *Gyn/Ecology*, London: The Women's Press.

Dench G (1992) *From extended family to state dependency*, London: Middlesex University.

Dench G (1994) *The Frog, the Prince and the Problem of Men*, London: Neanderthal.

Dench G, Flower T & Gavron K (eds) (1995) *Young at Eighty*, Manchester, Carcanet.

Dench G (1996a) *Transforming Men*, New Brunswick: Transaction.

Dench G (1996b) *The place of men in changing family culture*, London: Institute of Community Studies.

Dench G (ed) (1997) *Rewriting the sexual contract*, London: Institute of Community Studies. (1999 edition – New Brunswick: Transaction)

Dench G, Ogg J & Thomson K (1999) 'The role of grandparents', in Jowell R et al., (eds) *British Social Attitudes, the 16th Report*, Aldershot: Ashgate.

Dench G (ed) (2000) *Grandmothers of the Revolution*, London: Hera

Dench G & Ogg J (2002) *Grandparenting in Britain: a baseline study*, London: Institute of Community Studies.

Dench G (ed) (2002) *Grandmothers: Changing the Culture*, New Brunswick: Transaction.

Faludi S (1992) *Backlash*, London: Chatto & Windus.

Ferri E & K Smith (1996) *Parenting in the 1990s*, London: Family Policy Studies Centre.

Fisher H (1993) *Anatomy of Love*, New York: Simon & Schuster.

Gilder G (1973) *Sexual Suicide*, New York: Quadrangle.

Gilmore D (1990) *Manhood in the Making*, London: Yale University Press.

Hakim C (1997) *'Diversity and choice in the sexual contract: models for the 21st century'* in G Dench (1997).

Hrdy S B (1999) *Mother Nature*, London: Chatto & Windus.

James-Fergus S (1997) 'Rebuilding African-Caribbean families' in G Dench (1997)

Lloyd T (ed) (1996) *What next for men?* London: Working With Men.

Lyndon N (1992) *No more sex war*, Sinclair-Stevenson.

Madge C (1943) *War-time patterns of saving and spending*, Cambridge: NIESR.

Miles R (1986) *The Women's History of the World*, London: Michael Joseph.

Mooney B (1993) 'The year that sex began for me', *Sunday Times*, 21st March.

Morgan P (1995) *Farewell to the Family*, London: Institute of Economic Affairs.

Mount F (1982) *The Subversive Family*, London: Cape.

Neate P (2002) 'Where were you in the revolution, Granny?' in Dench G (ed) *Grandmothers: changing the culture*, New Brunswick: Transaction.

Nelson J (2002) 'Contemplating grandmotherhood' in Dench G (ed) *Grandmothers: changing the culture*, New Brunswick: Transaction.

Pateman C (1988) *The Sexual Contract*, Cambridge: Polity.

Platt J (1971) *Social Research in Bethnal Green*, London: Macmillan.

Rathbone E (1924) *The disinherited family*, London: Edward Arnold.

Secker S (2001) *For the sake of the children*, London: Families Need Fathers.

Snape P, Arthur S & Dench G (2002) *The moral economy of grandparenting*, London: National Centre for Social Research.

Young M (1951) *For Richer for Poorer*, Report to Labour Party Research Dept.

Young M (1952) 'Distribution of Income within the Family', *British Journal of Sociology*, vol. III, no. 4.

Young M (1954) 'The Planners and the Planned: the Family', *Journal of Town Planning Institute*, vol. XL, no. 3.

Young M (1958) *The Rise of the Meritocracy*, London: Thames & Hudson.

Young M & Syson L (1974) 'Women, the New Poor', *Observer*, 17th January.

Young M (1977) 'Towards a New Concordance', *New Society*, 17th November.

Young M (1990) '25 Years of the ESRC', *Social Sciences*, issue 7, HMSO.

Young M & Owen M (1992) *Campaign for Children's After-School Clubs*, Institute for Community Studies.

Young M & Halsey A H (1995) *Family and Community Socialism*, London: IPPR.

Young M & Willmott P (1957) *Family and Kinship in East London*, London: Routledge & Kegan Paul.

Young M & Willmott P (1960) *Family & Class in a London Suburb*, London: Routledge & Kegal Paul.

Young M & Willmott P (1973) *The Symmetrical Family*, London: Routledge & Kegan Paul.

Note on the author:

Geoff Dench is a research fellow at the *Institute of Community Studies* in London and at *University College, London*. He has been involved in research on family relations for the last ten years, and has written Transforming Men and edited Rewriting the Sexual Contract, both published by *Transaction* plus a number of reports on grandparenting. Before that his research was mainly on ethnic relations, in which he wrote Maltese in London, and Minorities in the Open Society, both published by *Routledge & Kegan Paul*. Until recently he was professor of sociology at *Middlesex University*.